Anonymus

The Rules of the Law Society of Upper Canada

Anonymus

The Rules of the Law Society of Upper Canada

ISBN/EAN: 9783741194320

Manufactured in Europe, USA, Canada, Australia, Japa

Cover: Foto ©Lupo / pixelio.de

Manufactured and distributed by brebook publishing software
(www.brebook.com)

Anonymus

The Rules of the Law Society of Upper Canada

THE

RULES

OF

THE LAW SOCIETY

OF

UPPER CANADA.

PASSED IN CONVOCATION, EASTER TERM,
52 VICTORIA,

AND APPROVED BY THE VISITORS OF THE
SOCIETY.

TORONTO:
PRINTED FOR THE SOCIETY BY ROWSELL & HUTCHISON.

1889.

The Law Society of Upper Canada.

Visitors.

THE HONOURABLE THE JUDGES OF THE SUPREME COURT OF JUDICATURE
FOR ONTARIO.

Treasurer.

HON. EDWARD BLAKE, Q.C.

Benchers.

Ex-Officio.

The ATTORNEY-GENERAL OF CANADA for the time being, and every person
who has held that office, if a member of the Bar of Ontario, and the
ATTORNEY-GENERAL for the time being of Ontario, and all Members
of the Bar of Ontario, who have at any time held the office of ATTOR-
NEY-GENERAL OF ONTARIO, or of ATTORNEY-GENERAL or SOLICITOR-
GENERAL for that part of the late Province of Canada formerly called
Upper Canada, and any retired JUDGE or JUDGES OF THE SUPERIOR
COURTS OF LAW AND EQUITY FOR ONTARIO OR OF THE SUPREME COURT
OF JUDICATURE FOR ONTARIO.

Elected.

(TO EASTER TERM, 1891.)

JOHN BELL, Q.C., Belleville.
JAMES BEATY, Q.C., Toronto.
BYRON MOFFAT BRITTON, Q.C., Kingston.
ALEXANDER BRUCE, Q.C., Hamilton.
HECTOR CAMERON, Q.C., Toronto.
JOSEPH HENRY FERGUSON, Toronto.
JAMES JOSEPH FOY, Q.C., Toronto.
HON. CHRISTOPHER FINLAY FRASER, Q.C., Brockville.
DONALD GUTHRIE, Q.C., Guelph.
HON. ARTHUR STURGIS HARDY, Q.C., Brantford.
JOHN HOSKIN, Q.C., Toronto.
ADAM HUDSPETH, Q.C., Lindsay.
ÆMILIUS IRVING, Q.C., Toronto.
NICOL KINGSMILL, Toronto.
JAMES KIRKPATRICK KERR, Q.C., Toronto.
ZEBULON AITON LASH, Q.C., Toronto.
D'ALTON McCARTHY, Q.C., Toronto.

THE BENCHERS OF THE LAW SOCIETY IN CONVOCA-
TION, IN TRINITY TERM, 1ST & 2ND WM. IV.,
PASSED THE FOLLOWING

RESOLUTIONS OF CONVOCATION.

1. *Resolved*—That the Law Society of Upper Canada was established by Act of Parliament of Upper Canada, the 27th Geo. III., chap. 13.

2. *Resolved*—That under that Act all persons duly entered of the Society and admitted on its Books, whether as Students or Barristers-at-Law, became by such entry and admission, to all intents and purposes whatsoever, Members of the Society.

3. *Resolved*—That by that Act the Society was empowered, with the approbation of the Judges of the Superior Courts as Visitors of the said Society, to make such Rules and Regulations as might be deemed necessary or proper for the government of the Society.

4. *Resolved*—That by a Rule of the Society of Michaelmas Term, 40th Geo. III., chap. 2, passed by the Society on the 9th day of November, 1799, at a general meeting summoned by letter to all the members, for the express purpose of altering and adding to the Rules and Regulations of the Society, and approved of by the Judges, according to the Statute, on the 16th day of January, 1800, it was provided that the Benchers of the Society for the time being should be considered Governors of the said Society, and have full power to make such Rules and Regulations from time to time as should or might be necessary for the welfare of the Society, subject to the inspection of the Judges.

5. *Resolved*—That by that rule the whole power of making Rules and Regulations for the government of the Society was duly transferred to and vested in the Convocation of Benchers.

6. *Resolved*—That by the Act of the Parliament of Upper Canada of 2nd Geo. IV., chap. 5, the Rule above mentioned and the proceedings of the Benchers under it were recognized and followed up by a legislative enactment incorporating that portion of the Society in which the power of legislating for the whole body had been so vested.

7. *Resolved*—That while this last-mentioned Act of Parliament confers corporate powers upon the Treasurer and Benchers only, under the corporate name of "The Law Society of Upper Canada," it does not interfere with the right of membership of persons duly entered of the Society and admitted on its books as Students or Barristers-at-Law, but leaves them members of the Law Society of Upper Canada, though not members of the Corporation of the Law Society of Upper Canada.

8. *Resolved*—That the powers conferred by this last-mentioned Act upon the Treasurer and Benchers, as well as all others with which they have been entrusted, are held by them in trust, and for the benefit of the Society at large, and not for the benefit of the Corporation of the Society only.

9. *Resolved*—That in fulfilling the various and important duties imposed upon it by the Constitution of the Society, the Convocation of the Benchers is frequently called upon to pass Rules for the government of the Society at large ; to adopt Resolutions explanatory of the sense entertained by the Benchers of existing regulations, and upon different other matters connected with the profession ; to make General Orders for the regulation of its own proceedings as a body ; and finally to direct by Particular Orders the executive business of the institution.

10. *Resolved*—That by the Act of Parliament of the 37th Geo. III., chap. 13, it is provided that the Rules and Regulations for the government of the Society shall be made with the approbation of the Judges, as Visitors of the Society.

11. *Resolved*—That the Judges have declined either to assent to, or dissent from resolutions of the Convocation, which did not contain provisions for the general government of the Society, expressly on the ground that their

authority as Visitors under the statute did not extend to control any such proceedings of the Convocation.

12. *Resolved*—That under the Act of Parliament of the 37th Geo. III. chap. 13, the approbation of the Judges is necessary only to the " Rules of the Society," that is, to such regulations as provide for the general government of the Society at large, or, as being general in their operation contain provision by which persons not members of the Convocation may be directly affected, and such are in no respect binding on the Society, or any member of it, until the Judges of the Province have duly approved thereof according to law.

13. *Resolved*—That, to " The Resolutions of the Convocation," that is, to such resolutions as are merely explanatory of the sense entertained by the Benchers, of existing rules or regulations, or upon other matters connected with the profession, the approbation of the Judges is in no wise necessary, but such are in every respect effectual for the purposes intended, and binding upon the Society at large, and upon every member thereof without such approbation.

14. *Resolved*—That to " The Standing Orders of the Convocation," that is, to such regulations of the Convocation as provide merely for the regulation of its own proceedings as a body, the approbation of the Judges is in no wise necessary, but such are in every respect effectual for the purposes intended, and binding upon the Society at large, and upon every member thereof without such approbation.

15. *Resolved*—That to " The Particular Orders of the Convocation," that is, to such orders as are given by the Convocation in directing the executive business of the Institution, the approbation of the Judges is in no wise necessary, but such are in every respect effectual for the purposes intended, and binding upon the Society at large, and upon every member thereof without such approbation.

THE RULES

PASSED BY

THE LAW SOCIETY OF UPPER CANADA,

WITH THE APPROBATION OF THE

JUDGES OF THE SUPREME COURT OF JUDICATURE

As Visitors of the said Society, so far as any of the foregoing Rules
is or are subject to Approval or Disapproval by the Visitors.

Finally passed in Convocation, Easter Term, 52 Victoria.

[8th June, 1889.]

By the Benchers of the Law Society of Upper Canada in
Convocation, with the approbation of the Judges of
the Supreme Court of Judicature for Ontario, as Visitors of the said Society, it is ordained as follows:

THE RULES.

1. The interpretation clauses of the Interpretation Acts
having force in Ontario, shall, so far as material and
applicable, be considered as also applying to the Rules
and Orders of the Society in like manner as if expressly
incorporated therewith.

2. All former Rules of the Society are hereby repealed.

THE SOCIETY.

3. The permanent seat of the Law Society shall be at
Osgoode Hall, in the City of Toronto.

4. The Seal of this Society heretofore in use, and
bearing the following device, viz.: a shield in the centre
whereof stands a doric column, surmounted by a beaver,
on the dexter side of the shield the figure of Her-
cules, and on the sinister, the figure of Justice, with the
scales in her right hand, and the sword in the left, and the
words, "*Magna Charta Angliæ*," inscribed on a ribbon
floating round the column, together with the words, " Law
Society of Upper Canada," upon the exterior circle, and
the words and figures, " Incorporated 1822." beneath the
column within the exterior circle, shall be. and shall continue to be, the Seal of the Society.

5. The custody of the Seal of the Society shall belong to the Treasurer for the time being, who shall countersign every instrument to which he shall affix such seal, and personally, or by the Sub-Treasurer, hand over the same to his successor.

6. The terms of the Society shall be as follows:— Hilary Term, commencing first Monday in February, lasting two weeks ; Easter Term, commencing third Monday in May, lasting three weeks ; Trinity Term, commencing second Monday in September, lasting two weeks; Michaelmas Term, commencing third Monday in November, lasting three weeks.

ROLLS AND OTHER ARCHIVES.

7. The Sub-Treasurer shall, during the term of his office, safely keep the rolls and archives of the Society.

8. No alteration or addition shall be made in or upon the rolls of the Society, except under the authority of Convocation.

9. At the close of every Term the entries to be made on the rolls in consequence of the admissions, calls, elections or appointments, or orders of Convocation during the Term, shall be thereupon made by the Sub-Treasurer in the paper roll and the index shall be continued, and the paper roll and index shall thereupon be submitted to the Committee on Journals and Printing for examination and approval.

10. The entries in the parchment rolls of the Society shall be made by the Sub-Treasurer from the paper roll, under the superintendence of the Committee on Journals and Printing.

CONVOCATION.

11. Any five Benchers shall be a quorum, except for the purpose mentioned in Rule 116.

12. In case a quorum of five Benchers should not be present at any meeting of Convocation, the Benchers present, (being not less than three), may, after the lapse of half an hour beyond the hour appointed for the meeting, proceed in the name and on behalf of the Society, to dispose of any application for admission on the books as a stu-

dent or articled clerk, or of any application for Call or
for Certificate of Fitness, by any person whose petition
stands regularly on the order of such day to be proceeded
with, and may dispose of such application as such Benchers may deem proper; and the action of such Benchers
thereon, shall have the like validity and effect as if the
same had been disposed of in full Convocation.

13. The Convocation of the Benchers shall be held at the
seat of the Society, in Term time, and on the last Tuesdays
in June and December, in vacation, unless such days be
holidays, when Convocation shall be held on the following
day. But Special Meetings of Convocation, in case of
emergency, may be convened in Vacation by the Treasurer,
upon the requisition of five members. A notice stating the
objects of the Special Meeting shall be sent by post to
each Bencher at least five days before the day of meeting.

14. The Treasurer may, if any unforseen emergency
render it necessary, summon a special meeting of Convocation for any day in Term time, by giving notice thereof
by telegraph or otherwise, and by fixing such notice in the
Library of the Society at least one day previous to the
day of meeting. (See form A in Appendix.)

15. Monday, Tuesday, and Saturday of the first week,
Friday of the second week, and Saturday of the third
week of Term shall be standing Convocation days, and
the hour of meeting, half-past ten o'clock in the forenoon,
unless otherwise ordered, and Convocation may adjourn,
from day to day, to any day previous to the next standing
Convocation day. The members of the Bench shall appear
in Convocation on the first and second days of meeting in
each Term in the costume of Barristers appearing in Court.

16. In default of a quorum after the lapse of thirty minutes beyond the hour of meeting, on any Standing Convocation day, or on any adjournment, the Treasurer, or in
his absence the Bencher being the senior Barrister present,
may adjourn the meeting of Convocation to any other day
in the same term, previous to the next standing Convocation day.

17. The proceedings of the Benchers in Convocation
shall be conducted as much as may be according to the
ordinary Parliamentary mode.

18. The Secretary shall report to Convocation on the first day of each Term, and at each meeting of Convocation held between Terms, the names of such elected Benchers, if any, as have failed to attend the meetings of Convocation for three consecutive Terms.

19. Such report shall then be referred to the Committee on Journals and Printing for report to Convocation thereon.

20. If such Committee report the seat of any Bencher vacant for the cause mentioned, a day shall be appointed for taking such report into consideration, and the Bencher interested shall be notified of the report and of the time at which it is to be taken into consideration.

21. No Draft Rule shall pass through more than two readings on the same day, but any Rule may pass through all its stages in the same Term, or be continued from Term to Term.

22. After any question is put, no further debate on the question shall be allowed, but the yeas and the nays shall be recorded at the request of any Bencher.

23. The Order of Proceedings at the ordinary meetings of Convocation shall be as follows :—

On the First Day of Term :

(1) Reading the Minutes of last Meeting of Convocation.

(2) Reports of the Examiners on the Examination of Candidates for Call, received, read, and approved, or otherwise disposed of.

(3) Secretary's Report on standing of Candidates.

(4) Call of Barristers in Convocation.

(5) Reports of the Examiners on the Examination of Candidates for admission as Attorneys, received, read, and approved, or otherwise disposed of.

(6) Reports of the Examiners on the Intermediate Examinations received.

(7) Reports of the Committee on Legal Education on Admissions of Students-at-Law and Articled Clerks, received and read.

(8) Reports of Standing or Special Committees received and read, and a time appointed for the consideration or adoption of the same.

(9) Petitions received, read and referred.

(10) Communications received, read and disposed of.

(11) Inquiries.

(12) Consideration of any other business specially appointed for the first Day of Term.

(13) Motions of which previous notice has been given.

(14) Notices of Motion.

(15) Second reading of draft Rules.

24. *On other Business Days of Convocation :*

(1) Reading the Minutes.

(2) Reports of Committees on Petitions respecting Call of Barristers, admission of Attorneys, or respecting Students or Clerks, or their Examinations, or on special Cases under Rules 206 to 213 inclusive ; and the consideration or the adoption of the same, and of the Reports of Examiners on the Intermediate Examinations.

(3) Reports of Standing or Special Committees, received, read, and a time appointed for the consideration or adoption of the same.

(4) Special Reports from the Examiners.

(5) Petitions received, read, and referred.

(6) Communications received, read, and disposed of.

(7) Inquiries.

(8) Consideration of any other business specially appointed for such day.

(9) Motions, of which previous notice has been given.

(10) Notices of motion.

(11) Second reading of draft Rules.

25. It shall be the duty of the Secretary, at each meeting of Convocation, to read the minutes of the previous

ordinary or special meeting, which, after being approved, shall be signed by the Treasurer, or the Chairman *pro tem.*

26. The proceedings of Convocation during each Term shall be printed under the superintendence of The Standing Committee on Journals and Printing.

27. An index to the Minutes of Convocation shall be prepared after each Term.

28. No petition praying for any special relief respecting fees, or the examination or period of study, of any Student-at-Law, or Candidate for Call, as Barrister ; or respecting the service, articles of clerkship, or examination of any articled clerk, or candidate for Certificate of Fitness ; or respecting any Admission into the Society or any Intermediate Examination, shall be considered by Convocation, until after having been referred to and reported upon by a Standing or Special Committee ; and every such petition (except a petition respecting fees, which is to stand referred to the Finance Committee) shall forthwith on its receipt by the Secretary, stand referred to the Legal Education Committee, and shall be transmitted by the Secretary to the Chairman of that Committee for its report.

STANDING COMMITTEES.

29. The following Standing Committees shall be annually elected on the first Saturday in Easter Term, and shall hold office until the appointment of their successors :—

1. Finance.
2. Library.
3. Reporting.
4. Legal Education.
5. Discipline.
6. Journals and Printing.
7. County Libraries Aid.

30. Each Standing Committee shall consist of nine members in addition to the Treasurer who shall be ex-officio a member of all Standing Committees, and three members of any Committee shall constitute a quorum, unless otherwise specially ordered.

31. Any Committee of Convocation may sit in Vacation as well as in Term time, and may adjourn from time to time.

32. Any vacancy in any Committee shall be filled up at the first business meeting of Convocation held after the occurrence of such vacancy.

THE TREASURER.

33. On the first Saturday in Easter Term, the second order shall be the Election of Treasurer pursuant to the Statute.

34. The Treasurer for the time being shall preside in Convocation.

35. In case of the absence of the Treasurer at any meeting, a Chairman, to preside in Convocation, shall be appointed by the Benchers present.

36. Such Chairman shall preside in Convocation at such meeting, and in all things officiate as Treasurer, during the absence of the Treasurer from Toronto, until the next meeting of Convocation.

37. In case of a vacancy in the office of the Treasurer, or of the Treasurer elect, before entering upon the duties of the office, the Benchers present at the first meeting of Convocation next ensuing the occurrence of such vacancy, shall, before proceeding to any other business, elect a Bencher to fill the office of Treasurer until the next statutory election.

OFFICERS.

38. There shall be the following salaried officers of the Society :

(1) A Secretary, who shall be ex-officio Sub-Treasurer and Librarian.

(2) An Editor who shall superintend the publishing of the Reports.

(3) A Reporter for the Court of Appeal for Ontario, four joint Reporters for the High Court of Justice for Ontario, and one Reporter of decisions on matters of Practice both in the Court of Appeal and in the High Court.

(4) A Principal of the Law School.

(5) Not less than two Lecturers in the Law School.

(6) Two Examiners.

(7) Two General Assistants who are to take their instructions from and obey the orders of the Secretary.

39. The officers above mentioned shall hold office during the pleasure of Convocation, and shall perform all such duties as may be assigned to them respectively by the rules of the Society, or by the Standing Orders, or by any special orders of Convocation.

40. No person shall be appointed an officer of the Society except after at least one week's notice by the Secretary, of the intention to appoint, given by circular to each Bencher; provided it shall, nevertheless, be competent for the Treasurer to temporarily fill any vacancies which the exigencies of the case may require to be filled.

41. Notwithstanding anything in Rule 38 contained, there shall be, during the incumbency of the present Reporter of the Court of Appeal, an Assistant Reporter for the said Court.

42. The salary of the Editor shall be two thousand dollars per annum.

43. The salary of each of the Reporters for the Court of Appeal and High Court shall be twelve hundred dollars per annum.

44. The salary of the present Reporter for the Court of Appeal shall be one thousand dollars per annum; the salary of the Assistant Reporter for the Court of Appeal shall be one thousand dollars per annum.

45. The salary of the Reporter for decisions on matters of Practice shall be nine hundred dollars per annum.

46. The salaries of the respective Reporters shall be payable monthly, but not without a certificate of the Editor that the work of the Reporter has been done to his satisfaction.

47. In case of the removal of any Reporter by the Society, his salary shall cease immediately upon his removal.

48. The salary of the Secretary shall be two thousand dollars per annum, payable monthly, for all his duties as Secretary, Sub-Treasurer, and Librarian, in addition to which he shall be furnished with rooms, fuel, water, and light.

49. The salary of one of the General Assistants shall be one thousand dollars per annum, and of the other General Assistant six hundred dollars per annum, payable monthly.

50. The salary of the Principal of the Law School shall be four thousand dollars per annum.

51. The salary of each of the Lecturers in the Law School shall not exceed eight hundred dollars per annum.

52. The salary of each of the Examiners shall not exceed five hundred dollars per annum.

THE SECRETARY.

53. In addition to the duties required of the Secretary by any Statute—

(1) He shall keep the minutes of the proceedings in Convocation, with a proper index thereto, and record the names of the Benchers present ; make up the journals, conduct all necessary correspondence, prepare all necessary diplomas, certificates, and other documents appertaining to his department, and perform all other services incidental to the office.

(2) He shall cause to be published in the *Canada Law Journal* as soon as may be after each Term :

    (*a*) The names of all Benchers elected or appointed during the previous Term.

    (*b*) The name of the Treasurer (if any) elected during such Term.

    (*c*) The names of all gentlemen upon whom the Degree of Barrister-at-Law was conferred during such Term, in the order of their Call.

(*d*) The names of all members admitted into the Society as Students-at-Law or Articled Clerks, during such Term, with the date, class, and order of their admission.

(*e*) Such portions of the Rules or Standing Orders of the Society respecting admission of Students-at-Law and the Examinations for Call to the Bar, and for Certificates of Fitness, specifying the subjects and books from time to time prescribed for such Examinations respectively, as shall be sufficient to give every necessary information to all parties interested in the premises.

(*f*) A *resumé* of the business of Convocation during Term, under the superintendence of the Journals Committee.

(3) He shall, forthwith after each Examination, post in a conspicuous place in the Library, a list, shewing the names of successful Candidates.

54. The Secretary, under the direction of the Finance Committee, shall have the general charge of the grounds and buildings thereon, which may be in the exclusive occupation of the Society.

55. The Secretary for the time being shall be required to give security by bond of some Guarantee Company to the Society to the extent of five thousand dollars, for the due performance of the duties of his office, including the duties of Sub-Treasurer, the Society to pay one-half the premium therefor.

56. The Secretary shall have his residence in the east wing of Osgoode Hall. No other persons except Officers or Servants of the Society, shall be permitted to reside in those portions of Osgoode Hall in the exclusive occupation of the Society.

FINANCE.

57. The Committee of Finance shall be charged with the management of the Finances of the Society, and all matters relating to its resources and expenditure, and may appropriate from time to time such sums as may be re-

quired for expenditure by other Standing Committees, and shall certify such other accounts as may be incurred, and order their payment.

58. Each Standing Committee charged with the management of business affecting the finances of the Society, shall annually prepare an estimate of the probable receipts and expenditure for the year in respect of its branch of the business. Such estimates shall be submitted to the Finance Committee during the Vacation prior to Hilary Term in each year, and the Finance Committee shall report thereon to Convocation with its own observations.

59. The whole executive management and control of those portions of Osgoode Hall, and the grounds attached thereto, in the exclusive occupation of the Society shall be vested in the Finance Committee, subject to the orders and supervision of the Benchers in Convocation.

60. The annual statement of receipts and expenditure shall be printed, and in accordance with R. S. O. cap. 145, sec. 53, a copy of such statement shall be sent by mail with the first number of the current Reports, to every practitioner who has taken out his certificates.

61. The Sub-Treasurer shall lay before the Finance Committee each month, a debit and credit statement of account of all moneys received up to and including the last day of the preceding month.

62. Such statement of account shall show all deposits made in the Bank of the Society to the credit of the Society, and all cheques drawn upon such Bank; and shall also show all disbursements made, and be accompanied by vouchers for the same.

63. Such accounts shall be audited monthly by a professional auditor appointed for that purpose.

64. A cash book shall be opened in which items of receipts and expenditure shall be extended in parallel columns, under several principal heads, from which they are to be posted into the Ledger under such heads.

65. The Bank of Toronto shall be the Bank of deposit and account for the Law Society of Upper Canada, and

the Sub-Treasurer shall from time to time deposit therein to the credit of the Society, all moneys received for and on account of the Society, which being done, such deposit shall exonerate the Sub-Treasurer making such deposit.

66. The moneys of the said Society, deposited in the said Bank, when required for the payment of salaries, contingencies, and other accounts from time to time required to be paid by the Rules or Orders of the Society, or by any Committee acting under or in accordance with any such Rules or Orders, shall be drawn and paid out upon cheques signed by the Treasurer, or by any other member of the Finance Committee who may be named by that Committee, and whose name and signature shall be furnished to the Bank by the Treasurer and Secretary, and such cheques shall always be countersigned by the Sub-Treasurer.

THE LIBRARY.

67. It shall be the duty of the Library Committee to assume the general supervision and management of the Library, and to purchase books therefor, as in their judgment may be necessary.

68. The Secretary shall have the immediate and general charge of the Library, under the superintendence of the Library Committee.

69. The Library Committee may expend annually in the purchase of books, for the use of the Library, such sum as may be recommended in the estimates to Convocation, and the Treasurer and Sub-Treasurer are hereby authorized to pay the amounts from time to time required by the Committee.

70. The following shall be the Standing Orders for the regulation of the Library :—

(1) The Library shall be kept open for the use of the members of the Law Society :

(a) During any sittings of the Courts and in Term time daily, except Sundays and Holidays, from nine o'clock, A.M., until five o'clock, P.M., or until the Courts rise, if sitting at five o'clock.

(*b*) In Vacation daily, except Saturdays, Sundays and
Holidays, from nine o'clock, A.M., until five
o'clock, P.M., except in the Long and Christmas
Vacations, when it shall be opened at ten o'clock,
A.M., and closed at three o'clock, P.M.

(*c*) On Saturdays it shall be opened at nine o'clock,
A.M., and closed at three o'clock, P.M.

(2) No conversation shall be carried on in the Library,

(3) No person shall bring his hat into the Library, nor
place his greatcoat, cloak, &c., on any table or chair
therein.

(4) No book shall be carried out of the Library, except
under the circumstances authorized by order of Convocation.

(5) It shall be the duty of every salaried officer of the
Society using a book, to restore it to its place in the
Library, immediately after using the same.

(6) It shall be the duty of the Librarian to enforce, and
to report to Convocation in Term any infringement of, the
Rules or Orders of the Society for the regulation of the
Library.

(7) It shall be the duty of the Librarian, under the
direction of the Library Committee, to procure and place
in the Library from time to time, the reports of the
Supreme Court of Judicature in England, and such other
books as the Committee shall order.

(8) The Judges of the Supreme Court of Judicature, the
Master in Chambers and the Master in Ordinary shall
be at liberty to take books from the Library, upon
application to the Librarian, and any member of the Law
Society requiring the use of any book upon the argument
of a case in Osgoode Hall, shall be at liberty to have
such book, upon application to the Librarian, such book
to be returned to its place in the Library immediately after
the close of the argument for which it may have been
required. Books taken from the Library in pursuance
of this rule are to be in all cases returned the same day ;
and any person taking any books from the Library other-

wise than upon such application, or failing to return the
same in the manner hereby directed, shall forfeit the benefit
allowed by this rule, until restored thereto by order of
Convocation or of the Treasurer.

(9) For the application to the Librarian mentioned in
the last sub-section, it shall be sufficient to enter the name
and volume of the book required and of the person taking
the same in a register book, which shall be kept in the
Library for that purpose.

(10) Text books of which duplicates are in the Library,
at least one copy of the latest edition being always
retained there, may be taken over night, to be returned
at the next morning's opening of the Library.

(11) Legal periodicals as follows:—*Albany Law Journal,
American Law Register, American Law Review, Book-
seller (The English), Canada Health Journal, Central Law
Journal, Criminal Law Magazine, Gibson's Law Notes,
Irish Law Times, Journal of Jurisprudence, Law Journal*
(English paper, not Law Journal Reports), *Law Magazine
and Review, Library Journal, Law Times* (English paper,
not Law Times Reports), *Legal News, Lower Canada
Jurist* (not Reports), *Law Quarterly Review* (Pollock),
Literary News, Solicitor's Journal, may be taken over
night, to be returned at the next morning's opening of the
Library.

(12) Books relating to literature other than legal literature, may be taken for a week; this definition is not to
include Books of Reference, Dictionaries and Encyclo-
pædias.

(13) The books named in sub-sections 10, 11 and 12
of this Rule shall be available only to Barristers and
Solicitors who are members of the Law Society, upon
application to the Librarian, whose duty it shall be to
issue them on such application, if the applicant shall
not have disregarded these rules previously; taking a
receipt on which shall be recorded the time of the return
of the book and its condition.

71. The Library shall be heated and lighted at the
expense of the Society, according to any arrangements
which may be from time to time made by the Committee
of Finance.

72. The County Court Judges of the Province of Ontario shall have the privilege of using the Benchers' rooms while at Osgoode Hall.

COUNTY LIBRARIES.

73. Until further ordered, Branch Law Libraries for the use of the Courts and the Profession may be established and maintained in any county town, or in exceptional cases in such other place in any county as Convocation may allow, on the following conditions :—

(1) To The County Libraries Aid Committee, shall stand referred all correspondence on the subject, and the Committee shall have power, subject to the directions of Convocation, to carry out the provisions of Rules 73 to 82 inclusive, so far as the Society is concerned ; the Finance Committee retaining its control over expenditure.

(2) The Practitioners in any county or union of counties may form a Library Association, under chapter 173 of the Revised Statutes of Ontario, by the name of "The (name of the county town or the county, or union of counties) Law (or Law Library) Association."

(3) It shall be provided by the Constitution of the Association:—

(*a*) That the Trustees thereof shall hold all the books thereof in trust, in case of the dissolution or winding-up of the Association, or the disposal of its property, to satisfy and repay to the Law Society all sums advanced by the Society to the Association.

(*b*) That a room for the custody and use of the books, and proper arrangements for their custody, shall be provided, if possible in the Court House.

(*c*) That the books shall be for the use of the Judges of the county and of those Practitioners who become members of the Association and pay the prescribed annual and other fees, and also for use, during Courts and hearings before the Local Master, of the Judges, and of all members of the Profession residing out of the county.

(*d*) That the prescribed annual and other fees shall not
exceed for those Practitioners who do not keep
offices in the county town, or in the town in
which the Library is kept, one-half of the amount
fixed for those who do keep offices in the county
town.

(*e*) That at least one-half of the said fees and the whole
of the aid at any time granted by the Law
Society, shall be applied in the purchase, binding,
and repairing of the books for the Library, and in
payment of the salary of a librarian or caretaker
to such an amount as may be approved of by the
County Libraries' Aid Committee.

(*f*) That the Association shall make an annual report
to the Law Society, shewing the state of its
finances, and of its Library for the fiscal year,
which shall commence on 1st January, and end
on 31st December of each year, with such other
particulars as may be required by the Standing
Committee.

(4) The Association shall transmit to the Law Society
proof of its Incorporation, and a copy of its declaration
and By-laws containing the above provisions, and proof
of the condition of its funds and Library, and proof
that it has acquired a suitable room therefor, with such
other particulars as may be required by the Standing
Committee.

74. The Standing Committee being satisfied that the
conditions above named have been complied with, may
report thereon to Convocation ; which may deal with
applications for aid as the state of the finances may permit, and Convocation shall see fit.

75. It being expedient to grant more liberal aid to
libraries during the early years after their institution, the
grant in aid from the Society shall be, for the initiatory or
first grant, an amount double the amount of the contribu-
tions in money actually paid, or of the value of books
actually given, from all local sources, such grant, however,
not exceeding a maximum sum of twenty dollars for each
practitioner in the county or union of counties ; and for
each year thereafter, an amount equal to the amount of the

fees actually paid to the Association by its members, such grant, however, not exceeding a maximum sum of five dollars in respect of each paid subscription.

76. All annual grants shall be payable within one month after the 31st day of December in each year, provided the required reports and information have been supplied within fifteen days thereafter, and provided that the association shall have taken due and proper care of the books, and shall have maintained and kept the Library in the Court House or other place approved of by Convocation, in a proper state of efficiency, and shall have in all other respects complied with the requirements of the Rules adopted from time to time by Convocation in relation to County Libraries ; and in case of default, the annual grant shall be suspended either in whole or in part, during such default, at the pleasure of Convocation.

77. Should the default aforesaid consist merely of delay in supplying the requisite reports and information, the annual grant may be paid within three months after the receipt thereof, if so ordered by the County Libraries and Finance Committees.

78. Whenever any Library Association, which has been established for two years and has regularly made the required return, and complied with the requirements of the rules, shall make it appear to the satisfaction of Convocation that such Association is unable to purchase such reports or text books as are necessary to make the library thoroughly efficient and useful, having regard to the locality in which the library is established, and the number of practitioners who are members thereof, Convocation may, on the report of the County Libraries Aid Committee, make a special grant either of books or money to such Association, or may advance, by way of a loan without interest, to such Association any sum not exceeding the estimated amount of the next three years' annual grants, and such loan shall be repaid out of future annual grants in such manner as Convocation shall direct ; provided that security shall be given to the satisfaction of Convocation for the due expenditure of any money grant or advance.

79. An Inspector of County Libraries shall be appointed by Convocation. The duty of the Inspector shall be to report to Convocation annually on the condition of the books in each library, the custody thereof, the fitness of the

4

rooms used for the Libraries, and the manner in which the Library is maintained, and such other matters as shall be required by the County Libraries Aid Committee or by Convocation, and the Inspector shall be paid such sum as Convocation may order for each annual report on each library.

80. Convocation may, in its discretion, authorize the payment of such proportion, (not exceeding two-thirds) of the salary of the librarian and of the expenses for telephone service of any Library Association which has been satisfactorily reported on by the Inspector, as Convocation may deem proper; Provided that in no case shall the grant to any Library Association under this Rule exceed the sum of two hundred dollars per annum.

81. Convocation may furnish to each Library such number of books for the use of Students as may be required, the books so furnished to be kept by the librarian of each Association, and Students to be allowed to use the same on similar conditions to those in force from time to time in regard to similar books at Osgoode Hall.

82. The Standing Committee shall report to Convocation on the first day of Hilary Term in each year, on the operations of the previous year.

ENCOURAGEMENT OF LEGAL STUDIES.

83. The County Libraries Aid Committee shall have power, subject to the direction of Convocation, to carry out the provisions of Rules 83 to 94 inclusive, for the encouragement of Legal studies, so far as the Law Society is concerned, and to that Committee all correspondence on the subject shall stand referred, the Finance Committee retaining its control over expenditure.

84. The members of the Law Society in every locality which contains a sufficient number, may form an organization by the name of " The (name of county town, county or union of counties) Legal and Literary Society," or some similar name.

85. Among the objects of the Association shall be the extension of the legal knowledge and the cultivation of the powers of reasoning, speech and composition of the members, by the delivery of lectures by barristers on some of the more important branches of the law, and examinations thereon, by the preparation and reading of essays, and by arguments on legal questions.

86. The Association may transmit to the Law Society proof of its formation, with a copy of its rules, and a list of its members, and proof that arrangements have been made for the delivery, during the season, of a course of eighteen or more lectures, at least one hour long, on three or more of rhe more important branches of the law, by three or more barristers, giving the subjects and the names of the lecturers, and proof that arrangements have been made for the holding, by two or more such lecturers, of a written examination, comprising twenty-four or more questions, equally divided among the various subjects of the lectures, such examination to be managed on the same general principles as are applied to the written examinations of the Law Society, subject to such modifications as the Standing Committee may, from time to time, direct. And the Association may thereupon apply to be recognized by the Law Society as an Association within the meaning of these Rules.

87. The Committee may require such further information and details as shall seem advisable, and may, on being satisfied as to the facts, resolve that the Association be recognized.

88. Any recognized Association may transmit to the Law Society proof that the course of lectures has been delivered to audiences comprising, on the average, twelve or more students ; and that the examination has been held, and that eight or more students have competed thereat ; and proof of the results of the examination.

89. In case it appears that any of the competitors have succeeded in obtaining at least three-quarters of the aggregate marks obtainable on all the subjects, and at least one-half of the aggregate marks obtainable in each subject, the first of such successful competitors shall be entitled to a prize of law books to the value of $25, the second to a like prize of the value of $15, and the third to a like prize of the value of $10.

90. The Standing Committee shall have power, on the application of any recognized Society, to authorize the division of the competitors into two classes, and the division of the prizes in the same way, under such regulations as may be made by the Committee ; and in that event prizes may be given to the value of $50 in each class.

91. The Osgoode Legal and Literary Society shall be deemed to be a recognized Society, within the meaning of this rule.

92. The Standing Committee may in any case require further information, or further evidence on any point connected with the proceedings.

93. The Standing Committee being satisfied that, under the above conditions, any competitor is entitled to a prize, may report thereon to the Finance Committee, stating the facts, and thereupon the Finance Committee may authorize the giving of the prize.

94. The Standing Committee shall report to Convocation on the first day of Hilary Term in each year on the operations of the previous year.

REPORTS.

95. The Reporting Committee shall see that the duties of the Reporters are discharged, and that the Reports are published in accordance with the Statutes and the Rules of the Law Society relating thereto, and shall report any default to Convocation.

96. The Secretary shall subscribe for eight copies of the Reports of the Supreme Court of Canada for the Osgoode Hall Libraries, and one copy for each of the County Libraries, to be supplied at the expense of the Society.

97. A copy of the Ontario Reports published by the Society, shall be supplied at the expense of the Society, to

(1) Each of the Judges of the Supreme Court of Canada, and the Judge of the Court of Exchequer.

(2) The Judges' Library of the Supreme Court of Canada.

(3) The Registrar of the Supreme Court of Canada.

(4) Each of the Judges of the Supreme Court of Judicature for Ontario, and any retired Judge.

(5) The Judges' Libraries of the Supreme Court of Judicature for Ontario.

(6) Each of the Judges of the County Courts in Ontario.

(7) Each Solicitor who has taken out his Certificates.

(8) Each of the County Libraries receiving aid from the Society, and an additional copy to each County Library where the County Law Association has fifty or more members who have paid their subscriptions, such additional copy to be supplied from and inclusive of the first volume of the present series of Appeal, Ontario, and Practice Reports, respectively.

(9) The Master in Chambers of the Supreme Court.

(10) The Master in Ordinary of the Supreme Court, the Registrar of the Chancery Division of the High Court of Justice, and any additional Official Referee of the High Court of Justice specially appointed under R. S. O. ch. 44, sec. 124, sub-sec. 2.

(11) The Master of Titles.

98. Upon paying fifteen dollars to the Secretary during Michaelmas Term of any year, any Barrister-at-Law, not in arrears in the payment of his Bar fees, and not entitled under Rule 97, sub-section 7, or any Student or Articled Clerk, shall become entitled to receive the numbers of the Ontario Reports, the Ontario Appeal Reports, and the Ontario Practice Reports published by the Society during the ensuing year, in the same manner as Solicitors who have taken out their certificates.

99. It shall be the duty of the Editor to determine what decisions ought to be published, to peruse and settle the reports thereof prepared by the Reporters, and to superintend the preparation and publication of such decisions. He is also to make such arrangements with the Judges and officers of the Courts that reports of all important decisions may be secured to the profession ; and he shall oversee the whole work of reporting, so as to secure its efficient and prompt execution.

100. It shall be the duty of Reporters to attend their respective Courts personally, and to prepare a report of each important case, including the arguments of counsel, the authorities cited, and the judgment (whether oral or written), and to furnish the same without delay to the Editor

101. It shall also be the duty of the Reporters, under the direction of the Editor, to deliver the reports in fair legible

manuscript to the printers, to read and correct the proof, and to see them through the press with despatch.

102. It shall also be the duty of the Reporters to prepare and furnish short notes of all important decisions for early publication, under such regulations as may from time to time be made by Convocation.

103. In case of the unavoidable absence of any of the said Reporters from illness or any other sudden or necessary cause, during any of the sittings of the said several and respective Courts, it shall be competent for such Reporter so absent, with the assent of the Treasurer of the Society, to appoint for the time being some fit and proper person, being a Barrister-at-Law practising in the Court, to report the judgments to be reported by the said Reporter.

104. Each of the Reporters of the said respective Courts shall be responsible for the due discharge of such duties by such his nominee as aforesaid.

105. It shall at all times be competent for the Benchers in Convocation, in their discretion, to grant leave of absence to the said respective Reporters for such periods, and under such restrictions and conditions for ensuring the due performance of the duties of the office during such absence, as to the said Benchers in Convocation may seem expedient.

106. Every report shall state the short style of the action or proceeding, the Judge or Judges who presided, the Counsel and Solicitors for the parties, and the date of the argument, and of the judgment.

107. The reports shall be issued in three series, in volumes to be numbered consecutively. The first series shall consist of decisions of the Court of Appeal, and shall be called "The Ontario Appeal Reports"; the second shall consist of decisions of the High Court of Justice and shall be called "The Ontario Reports"; and the third shall consist of decisions in the Court of Appeal and in the High Court of Justice, on questions of practice, and shall be called "The Ontario Practice Reports."

108. The Appeal and Practice Reports respectively shall be issued as nearly as possible in monthly numbers, and

the Ontario Reports in semi-monthly numbers, but so
that no case shall remain unpublished for more than two
months after judgment ; and the volumes shall be of the
same size and style as heretofore, with index and digest.

109. The Reporters of the Court of Appeal and of the
High Court of Justice, shall report Election Decisions
under the direction of the Editor.

110. This work shall be distributed among the Reporters,
as they may arrange between themselves, or as may be
prescribed by the Editor in advance of the trials.

111. It shall not be necessary for the Reporters to
attend trials personally, but they shall take care to procure from the Judges, Registrars, Counsel, and short-hand
writers, engaged in the respective trials, the materials for
a report.

112. The Practice Reporter shall prepare reports of all
decisions on questions of practice in Election Cases pro-
nounced elsewhere than at the trial.

113. Election Decisions, including those on points of
Practice, shall be published in volumes as may be directed
by the Editor, with the approval of the Reporting Committee.

114. The Editor and Reporters shall also prepare and
publish a Triennial Digest of the Reports published by the
Society, including appeals from Ontario to the Supreme
Court of Canada, and the Privy Council. The materials
for the Digest shall be prepared *pari passu* with the
Reports, so that it may be published promptly at the end
of each triennial period.

115. In the event of any Reporter being requested by
any person to furnish a copy in writing of any Judgment,
delivered in the Court of which he is a Reporter, before the
publication thereof as hereby required, it shall be the duty
of such Reporter to furnish such copy in writing to the
person demanding the same with as convenient despatch
as possible, upon receiving the sum of ten cents per folio
of one hundred words of such Judgment, which sum, and
no more, such Reporter is hereby authorized to charge and
receive ; but no such charge shall be made in the case of
a copy in writing being required of any such Judgment

after the expiration of two months from the delivery thereof, but if not previously published, such copy shall be then furnished *gratis* by such Reporter to the party demanding the same.

DISCIPLINE.

116. Whenever any complaint shall be made to the Law Society, charging any barrister, solicitor, student, or articled clerk with misconduct as defined by R. S. O. chap. 145, secs. 44 to 47, such complaint shall be reduced to writing, and shall be submitted to Convocation at its next meeting, and in case Convocation shall be of opinion that a *prima facie* case has been shewn, the matter shall be sent to the Discipline Committee for investigation ; and' the said Committee shall thereupon send a copy of the complaint to the party complained of, and shall notify in writing the complainant and party against whom the complaint has been made, of the time and place appointed for such investigation ; and the said Committee shall, at the time and place appointed, proceed with the investigation, and shall reduce to writing the statements made and evidence adduced by the parties, or such of them as shall appear pursuant to such notice, and shall submit the same, together with all books and papers relating to the matter, with their views thereon, to Convocation, which shall take such action thereon, as to Convocation shall seem just and meet ; provided that no Barrister shall be disbarred, nor Attorney deprived of his certificate, except by a two-thirds majority of Benchers then present in Convocation, which, for the purpose aforesaid, shall consist of not less than fifteen members.

117. In case the parties or any of them fail to appear pursuant to notice at the time and place appointed, the said Committee may thereupon proceed with said investigation in their absence.

118. It shall be competent for Convocation to refer any such complaint to the Discipline Committee to consider and report whether a *prima facie* case has been shown.

119. Upon any order being made by the Court of Appeal for Ontario or any of the Divisions of the High Court of Justice for Ontario, whereby any person being at the time a member of this Society is ordered to be struck off the

Roll of Solicitors, and whereby it is also further ordered that such order shall be transmitted by the proper officer of such Court to the Treasurer of this Society, such person so ordered to be struck off the Rolls shall, *ipso facto*, be suspended from the exercise of all and singular the rights, powers, and privileges belonging to him in this Society, or elsewhere, as a member thereof, and such suspension shall continue until such person be restored to the Rolls as a Solicitor.

120. Such suspension shall in no respect be deemed as affirmation on the part of this Society, or any of the authorities thereof, of the correctness of the grounds upon which the decision of such Court or Courts is founded, but as a mere legal consequence attaching to such decision.

121. Such suspension shall not preclude the adoption of proceedings by impeachment or otherwise, according to the course of the Society, before the Benchers thereof in Convocation, for disbarring and expelling such person from the Society, on the same grounds upon which any such Court may have proceeded to remove him from their Rolls, or on any other ground that may render such proceedings necessary or proper in that behalf.

122. It shall be the duty of the Treasurer on receipt of any such order from the proper officer of any of the said Courts, to lay the same before Convocation at its next meeting ; and the same shall be thereupon entered at length upon the Journals of Convocation, but no entry of such suspension shall be entered upon the Rolls of the Society.

123. The Secretary shall, after the entry upon the Journals of Convocation of the order of any of the said Courts ordering a member of the Society to be struck off the Roll of Solicitors, notify by letter each of the Judges of the said Courts, and the Judges of the County Courts of the Counties in which the member of the Society affected by such order has practised, and also the said member himself, that the said order has been made and transmitted to the Treasurer of the Society.

124. Upon the Treasurer being informed of any order having been made by any of the said Courts for the restoration of such person to the Rolls, it shall be his

5

duty to procure an office copy of such order so restoring
such person to the Rolls and to lay the same before
Convocation at its next meeting, and the same shall
thereupon be entered at length upon the Journals of
Convocation.

125. In every matter in which application shall be made
to any of the Courts, or to any of the Judges thereof,
against a Solicitor for misconduct, the Reporters shall give
in their Reports the style of the matter and name of the
Solicitor, if a rule or motion be made absolute therein
against the Solicitor for such misconduct.

ADMISSION.

The mode of admission upon the books of the Society
of Students-at-law and Articled Clerks, shall be as
follows:

126. The Legal Education Committee shall superintend
the admission of Candidates as Students-at-Law and
Articled Clerks, and shall report to Convocation during
Term, upon admissions, in the manner hereinafter provided with regard to Examinations.

127. Three of the said Committee shall be a quorum for
the transaction of business.

128. Students-at-Law and Articled Clerks shall be
admitted during Easter and Trinity Terms only.

129. No person shall be admitted as a Student-at-Law
or as an Articled Clerk, who is not of the full age of sixteen
years.

130. Notice of the intention of any person to apply for
admission as a Student-at-Law or as an Articled
Clerk, signed by a Bencher, and containing the name,
addition and family residence of the Candidate, must be
delivered to the Secretary of the Society, at his office in
Osgoode Hall, on or before the fourth Monday preceding
the Term in which he seeks admission. (See Form B.
in the Appendix.)

131. The Secretary shall, as soon as the time for receiving notices has expired, make out two lists containing the names, additions, and family residences of all the Candidates, for whose admission notices of presentation have been regularly given, and shall affix one of such lists in a conspicuous place in his office, and the other in the Convocation Hall.

132. A Graduate in the Faculty of Arts in any University in Her Majesty's Dominions, empowered to grant such Degrees, shall be entitled to admission on the books of the Society as a Student-at-law or Articled Clerk, without further examination by the Society, upon giving the said notice, and paying the prescribed fees, and presenting his Diploma or a proper Certificate of his having received his Degree.

133. Any such Graduate who has given the said notice, and has otherwise complied with the rules of the Society, may, upon presenting to Convocation, at its meeting on the last Tuesday in June in any year, his diploma or a proper certificate of his having received his degree, be admitted on the books of the Society as a Student-at-law or Articled Clerk, and such admission shall be taken to be as on the first Monday of Easter Term.

134. The notice required by Rules 132 and 133 may be given within three months prior to the Graduate taking his degree.

135. A Student of any University in this Province, who shall present a Certificate of having passed, within four years of his application, an Examination in the subjects prescribed by Convocation for the time being, shall be entitled to admission as a Student-at-law, or as an Articled Clerk (as the case may be), without further examination by the Society, on giving the said notice, and paying the prescribed fee.

136. Graduates and Matriculants of Universities respectively shall be classed according to their rank, if Graduates or Matriculants of the same University ; or according to the dates of their diplomas or degrees, or certificates, if Graduates or Matriculants of different Universities.

137. Personal attendance of any applicant for admission as a Student or Clerk shall be dispensed with.

138. The Candidate must be presented by a writing, signed by a Barrister of the Ontario Bar, in a form approved of by Convocation. (See Form C in Appendix.)

139. Every Candidate for admission shall, some convenient time previous to the Term in which he seeks admission, deposit with the Sub-Treasurer at Osgoode Hall, his presentation and the amount of fees payable on admission, together with his petition for admission, which presentation and petition respectively shall be in the terms, and shall contain the information, required by the forms C and D contained in the Appendix ; and every Candidate for admission as Articled Clerk only, shall do the like ; his forms of presentation and petition, however, are to be varied to suit his case.

140. The first day of Term shall be taken to be the admission day of Students-at-Law and Articled Clerks who have been reported as admitted by the Committee during such Term, although the report may not have been presented to Convocation upon the first day of the Term.

141. The Fees payable shall be as follows With notice of intention to apply for admission, one dollar , on presentation for admission as Student-at-Law, fifty dollars, and as Articled Clerk, forty dollars.

(*a*) Any person who has been admitted as an Articled Clerk, on subsequently, within five years thereafter, applying for admission as Student-at-Law, shall pay, instead of fifty dollars, the sum of ten dollars.

SERVICE.

142. Except in special cases provided for by any Statute, Students-at-Law who are not Articled Clerks shall actually and *bona fide* attend in a Barrister's chambers for the same respective periods as Articled Clerks are required to serve under Articles.

143. The Term of attendance or of service under Articles shall be effectual only from the date of admission.

144. No person attending in the Chambers of a Barrister in pursuance of Rule 142, shall, during his term of attendance, hold any office of emolument, or engage or be employed in any occupation whatever, other

than that of Student in attendance, and no person bound by articles of clerkship to any Solicitor, shall, during the term of service mentioned in such articles, hold any office of emolument, or engage or be employed in any occupation whatever, other than that of Clerk to such Solicitor, or his partner, or partners (if any) and his Toronto Agent, with the consent of such Solicitors, in the business, practice or employment of a Solicitor (For Form of Articles of Clerkship, *see* Appendix M.)

THE LAW SCHOOL.

145. The Legal Education Committee shall have power to make Regulations, not inconsistent with these Rules, with respect to all matters relating to the proper working of the Law School, and the carrying out of all matters incidental to the Rules relating thereto, which Regulations shall be reported to Convocation at its first meeting after the making thereof.

146. The Law School established in Michaelmas Term, 1881, is continued upon the basis established by these rules.

147. The staff of the Law School shall consist of (*a*) a Principal, who shall be a Barrister of not less than ten years standing. (*b*) Not less than two Lecturers. (*c*) Two Examiners.

148. No person, while holding the office of Lecturer, shall be appointed or act as Examiner.

149. The Principal shall, in addition to the duty of lecturing and the discharge of such other duties as may be assigned to him by Convocation, have supervision and general direction of the School, and shall engage in no professional work other than that of consulting counsel ; nor shall he be a member of any firm of practising Barristers or Solicitors ; and he shall reside in or near Toronto.

150. Subject to the approval of the Legal Education Committee, the Principal shall arrange the subjects and books for lectures, the branches to be treated upon by each Lecturer, and the days and hours for lectures and discussions in the School during the School term.

151. The duties of the Lecturers shall be to deliver *viva voce* lectures, to superintend classes, prepare questions for classes, and, under the superintendence of the Principal, to

perform such other duties as may be assigned to them by the Principal.

152. The duties of the Examiners shall be to prepare all questions for, and to conduct and report to Convocation upon, all examinations whether written or oral, and to perform such other duties as may be assigned to them by Convocation.

153. The Course in the School shall be a three years course, and shall consist of Lectures, Discussions and Examinations.

154. The School term shall commence on the fourth Monday in September, and shall close on the first Monday n May ; with a Vacation commencing on the Saturday before Christmas and ending on the Saturday after New Year's Day.

155. A Student must complete the course of study of the First Year, and pass the Examination thereon at the close of the School term, before he enters on the Second Year; and must complete the course of study of the Second Year, and pass the Examination thereon at the close of the School term, before he enters on the Third Year.

156. Subject to the special provisions hereinafter contained respecting Students-at-Law and Articled Clerks now on the books, the attendance in the School shall be compulsory, as follows : All Students-at-Law or Articled Clerks must, during the last two years of their attendance in chambers or service under Articles, attend the School terms in the second and third years of the School Course respectively. Students-at-Law or Articled Clerks who, during the last three years of their attendance or service, are in attendance or under service in Toronto during three School terms, must attend in the School during such terms, the School years being taken in consecutive order of first, second, and third years. In the case of Graduates the last three years of attendance or service shall mean the whole three years of attendance or service.

157. Where any University of the Province has established a Law Faculty, and provided for a course of instruction and lectures thereat, similar to those adopted at the Law School, and to the satisfaction of Convocation, the attendance of a Student-at-Law or Articled Clerk upon

such course of instruction and lectures shall be accepted in lieu of the like attendance upon the first year of the School Course.

158. The School term, if duly attended by a Student-at-Law or Articled Clerk, shall be allowed as part of the term of attendance in chambers or service under articles.

159. Each Student-at-Law and Articled Clerk shall pay in advance a fee of $10 for each term of the Course which he shall attend.

160. All Students-at-Law and Articled Clerks who are Graduates, and who, at the date of the coming into force of these Rules, have entered upon the second year of their course, shall be exempt from the operation of these Rules in so far as they require attendance in the School.

161. All Students-at-Law and Articled Clerks in attendance or under service in Toronto, who are Graduates, and who, at the date of the coming into force of these Rules, have not entered upon the second year of their course, shall attend at least one term in the School, in the third year of the School Course.

162. All Students-at-Law and Articled Clerks who are not Graduates, and who, at the date of the coming into force of these Rules, shall have entered upon the fourth year of their course, shall be exempt from the operation of these Rules in so far as they require attendance in the School.

163. All Students-at-Law and Articled Clerks in attendance or under service in Toronto, who are not Graduates, and who, at the date of the coming into force of these Rules, are in the third year of their course, shall attend at least one term in the School, in the third year of the School Course.

164. All Students-at-Law and Articled Clerks in attendance or under service in Toronto, who are not Graduates, and who, at the date of the coming into force of these Rules, are in the second year of their course, shall attend at least two terms in the School, in the second and third years respectively of the School Course.

165. All Students-at-Law and Articled Clerks in attendance or under service elsewhere than in Toronto, and who were admitted prior to Hilary Term, 1889, shall be exempt from the operation of these Rules in so far as they require attendance in the School.

166. All other Students-at-Law and Articled Clerks shall be subject to these Rules.

167. Any Student-at-Law or Articled Clerk may attend any term in the School, upon payment of the prescribed fees.

EXAMINATIONS.

168. Examinations shall be held during the two weeks which commence on the first Monday in May, and during the week which commences on the first Monday in September. Such examinations shall include the work of the School during the preceding School term, and such other subjects as may be prescribed.

169. The Examinations which include the work of the First and Second Years of the School Course respectively, shall be the First and Second Intermediate Examinations, respectively. The Examination which includes the work of the Third Year of the School Course shall be the Examination for Call to the Bar and admission as Solicitor. The Examinations shall include the work of the Course, and such other subjects as may be prescribed.

170. The Legal Education Committee shall superintend all Examinations.

171. The Committee shall have power to arrange Examinations for Students-at-Law and Articled Clerks now on the books of the Society and by these rules exempted from attendance in the school in whole or in part, so as to enable them to proceed to call and admission as heretofore.

172. The Committee shall, on the first day of Term next after any Examination, report to Convocation the result of such Examination, specifying the names of those who have passed, and those who have been rejected, and the order in which those passed have been classed ; and such report shall be final.

173. Every Student-at-Law or Articled Clerk who has passed any Examination, shall be entitled to receive a certificate from the Secretary to that effect on payment of the fee therefor.

174. The ordinary Examinations prescribed for Call to the Bar, shall be passed in all cases where special Acts of the Legislature are obtained for such Call, with clauses requiring examination by the Society.

CALL AND CERTIFICATE.

The rules regulating Call to the Bar and admission as Solicitor, shall be as follows :

175. No Student-at-Law upon the books of this Society shall be called to the Bar until he shall have been five years, or, if admitted on the Books of this Society as a Graduate, three years, upon the Books ; and no Candidate shall be called to the Bar or receive a Certificate of Fitness, unless he be of the full age of twenty-one years, nor without having been previously examined.

176. Every Candidate for Call to the Bar, must cause a written notice in the form approved of by the Society, signed by a Bencher, of his intention to present himself for Call, to be given to the Secretary at his office in Osgoode Hall, on or before the fourth Monday preceding the Term in which he intends so to present himself. (Appendix F.)

177. The Secretary shall, as soon as the time for receiving notices has expired, make out two lists, containing the names, additions and residences of all the Candidates for Call, on behalf of whom notices of presentation have been regularly given, and shall affix one of such lists in a conspicuous place in his office, and the other in Convocation Hall.

178. The Secretary shall, on the first day of Term, make a report in writing to Convocation, stating—

(1) That notice of Presentation has been properly given for the Candidate.

(2) The date of admission of the Candidate.

6

(3) Whether the Candidate was admitted as a Graduate or Matriculant, and

(4) That the Intermediate Examinations have been passed by the Candidate, giving the dates thereof.

179. Every Candidate for Call to the Bar must be presented to Convocation by an instrument in writing, signed by a Barrister of Ontario, (see Form G in Appendix), and shall, previous to his Call to the Bar, give a bond to the Corporation in the penal sum of four hundred dollars, with two responsible sureties to be approved of by the Sub-Treasurer, with a condition in the terms and to the effect of form H and with a certificate in the form I contained in the Appendix.

180. Every Candidate shall, on or before the third Saturday preceding the Term in which he desires to be called, deposit with the Sub-Treasurer his bond presentation, and also his petition for Call (Appendix J.), which petition shall contain a statement of his age, of the day on which the period of his standing on the books, necessary to entitle him to be called to the Bar, expired or will expire, the Intermediate Examinations he has passed, and the names of the persons under whose superintendence he has received his professional education, according to the form J contained in the Appendix, and shall also, at the same time and place, deposit the amount of fees payable on being called.

181. The Sub-Treasurer's receipt for such fees shall be sufficient to entitle the Candidate to appear before the Examiners, and to be by them examined for Call, although the period of standing on the books entitling such Candidate to present himself shall not expire until a date during the ensuing Term.

182. Every Candidate for Call to the Bar who has not served under Articles shall, with his petition for Call, leave with the Sub-Treasurer of the Society at Osgoode Hall, answers to the several questions set forth in the Schedule "A" of this Rule, and also answers to the questions set forth in the Schedule "B" of this Rule, signed by the Barrister in whose Chambers such Candidate has attended in pursuance of Rule 142, together with the certificate in the said last mentioned Schedule also contained.

Schedule "A."

The following questions are to be answered by the Candidate himself:

1st. What was your age at the date of your admission?

2nd. Have you actually and *bona fide* attended during your whole term of years in the Chambers of some Barrister? If so, give the name and address of such Barrister. And if not, state the reason.

3rd. Have you, at any time during the said term, been absent without permission of the Barrister in whose Chambers you attended? And if so, state the length and occasion of such absence.

4th. Have you, during the period of your attendance, been engaged or concerned in any profession, business, or employment other than your professional employment as Student in attendance?

5th. Have you, since the expiration of your said term, been engaged or concerned, and for how long a time, in any, and what, profession, trade, business, or employment, other than the profession of a Barrister?

Schedule "B."

The following questions are to be answered by the Barrister or Barristers in whose Chambers the Student has attended, for any part of his term:

1st. Has A. B. actually and *bona fide* attended during his whole term of years in your Chambers? And if not, state the reason.

2nd. Has the said A. B., at any time during the said term, been absent without your permission? and if so, state the length and occasion of such absence.

3rd. Has the said A. B., during the said term, been engaged or concerned in any profession, business, or employment other than his professional employment as Student in attendance?

4th. Has the said A. B., during the whole term, with the exceptions above-mentioned, been faithfully and diligently employed in your professional business of a Barrister?

5th. Has the said A. B., since the expiration of his said term, been engaged or concerned, and for how long a time, in any, and what, profession, trade, business, or employment other than the profession of a Barrister?

6th. And I do hereby certify that the said A. B. has actually and *bona fide* attended in my Chambers for the period of — ; and that he is a fit and proper person to be called to the Bar.

183. No Candidate for Call who shall have omitted to leave his petition and all his papers and fees with the Sub-Treasurer, on or before the third Saturday preceding the term, as by the rules required, shall be called except after report upon a petition by him presented, praying relief on special grounds, subject however to the next succeeding Rule.

184. In case any such Candidate at the time of leaving his petition and papers with the Sub-Treasurer of the Society as hereinbefore provided, proves to the satisfaction of the said Sub-Treasurer, that it has not been in his power to procure the answers to the questions contained in the said Schedule " B" from the Barrister in whose Chambers he may have attended during any part of the time, or the Certificate therein also contained, the said Sub-Treasurer shall state such circumstances specially in his report to Convocation on such Candidate's petition.

185. Every member of the Society on the Common Roll being a Candidate for Call to the Bar shall, when passed, be admitted to the Degree of Barrister in the order of his precedence on the Common Roll, unless Convocation, at the time of his Examination being passed, otherwise order, and every candidate who petitions for Call to the Bar by virtue of his having been called to any other Bar, shall, when called, take precedence next after the members of the Society of longer standing on the books called upon the same day.

186. Every Gentleman, upon his being called to the Bar, shall appear before Convocation in the costume of a

Barrister appearing in Court, for the purpose of his being presented to the Superior Courts; and he may be so presented by any Bencher present in Court.

187. The Diploma of Barrister-at-Law of the Society, shall be in the Form K. in the Appendix.

188. All applications for Certificates of Fitness for admission as a Solicitor shall be by petition (Appendix L.) addressed to the Benchers of the Society in Convocation, and every such petition, together with the documents required by the Act, and the fees payable to this Society thereunder, or under the rules of the Courts, or those of the Society, shall be left with the Sub-Treasurer of the Society at Osgoode Hall, on or before the third Saturday next before the Term in which such petition is to be presented, and the Sub-Treasurer's receipt for such fees shall be sufficient authority to the Examiners to examine the applicant, although the Term of service of such applicant shall not expire until a date during the ensuing Term.

189. Every Candidate for a Certificate of Fitness as a Solicitor, and every Candidate for Call to the Bar only, who has served under Articles in pursuance of Rule 142, shall, with his petition for Certificate or Call, as the case may be, leave with the Sub-Treasurer of the Society at Osgoode Hall, answers to the several questions set forth in the Schedule " A " of this Rule, and also answers to the questions set forth in the Schedule " B " of this Rule, signed by the Solicitor with whom such Candidate has served his clerkship, together with the Certificate in the said last mentioned Schedule also contained.

Schedule " A."

The following questions are to be answered by the Clerk himself

1st. What was your age at the date of your articles?

2nd. Have you served the whole term of your articles at the office where the Solicitor or Solicitors to whom you were articled or assigned carried on his or their business? And if not, state the reason.

3rd. Have you, at any time during the term of your articles, been absent without permission of the Solicitor or Solicitors to whom you were articled or assigned? And if so, state the length and occasion of such absence.

4th. Have you during the period of your articles, been engaged or concerned in any profession, business or employment other than your professional employment as Clerk to the Solicitor or Solicitors to whom you were articled or assigned?

5th. Have you, since the expiration of your articles, been engaged or concerned, and for how long a time, in any, and what, profession, trade, business or employment, other than the profession of a Solicitor (or Barrister, as the case may be)?

Schedule " B."

The following questions are to be answered by the Solicitor or his Agent with whom the Clerk may have served any part of the time under his articles :

1st. Has A. B. served the whole term of his articles at the office where you carry on your business? And if not, state the reason.

2nd. Has the said A. B., at any time during the term of his articles, been absent without your permission? and if so, state the length and occasion of such absence.

3rd. Has the said A. B. during the period of his articles, been engaged or concerned in any profession, business, or employment other than his professional employment as your articled clerk?

4th. Has the said A. B., during the whole term of his clerkship, with the exceptions above-mentioned, been faithfully and diligently employed in your professional business of a solicitor?

5th. Has the said A. B., since the expiration of his articles, been engaged or concerned, and for how long a time, in any, and what, profession, trade, business, or employment other than the profession of a Solicitor, (or Barrister, as the case may be)?

6th. And I do hereby certify that the said A. B. has duly and faithfully served under his articles of clerkship (or assignment as the case may be) bearing date, &c., for the term therein expressed ; and that he is a fit and proper person to be admitted as a Solicitor, (or Barrister, as the case may be.)

190. No Candidate for Certificate of Fitness who shall have omitted to leave his Petition and all his papers and fees with the Sub-Treasurer, on or before the third Saturday preceding the Term, as by the Rules required, shall be admitted, except after report upon a Petition by him presented, praying relief on special grounds, subject however to the next succeeding Rule.

191. In case any such Candidate at the time of leaving his petition for Certificate of Fitness and papers with the Secretary of the Society as hereinbefore provided, proves to the satisfaction of the said Secretary, that it has not been in his power to procure the answers to the questions contained in the said schedule " B," or the Certificate of Service therein also contained, from the Solicitor with whom he may have served any part of the time under his articles, or from his agent, the said Secretary shall state such circumstances specially in his report to Convocation on such Candidate's petition (see following Rule.)

192. The Secretary shall report upon the petition of every Candidate for Certificate of Fitness, and such report, together with the petitions and documents to which they refer, shall be laid on the table of Convocation on the first day of Term ; he shall also make a Supplementary Report upon the articles of clerkship when received by him, of applicants, either for Certificates of Fitness or for Call only, whose term of service expires during Term.

193. In the computation of time entitling Students or Articled Clerks to pass Examinations to be called to the Bar or receive Certificate of Fitness. Examinations passed before or during Term shall be construed as passed at the actual date of the Examination, or as of the first day of Term, whichever shall be most favourable to the Student or Clerk.

194. Any person who, having entered the Society as a Student-at-Law, has proceeded regularly to the degree of

Barrister-at-Law, and who thereafter serves under Articles for the full Term during which he would, if an Articled Clerk only, have been required to serve, shall, upon completing his Articles, and petitioning under the foregoing Rules for a Certificate of Fitness, be entitled to have allowed to him the Intermediate Examinations passed by him when proceeding to the degree of Barrister-at-Law.

195. Applicants for Certificates of Fitness of the class contemplated by section 4 of chapter 147 of the Revised Statutes of Ontario, shall be examined on the statute laws of the Province of Ontario, including the Judicature Act, and the Consolidated Rules of Practice, before a Committee of Benchers to be appointed by Convocation; and, upon passing such Examination, they shall be reported to the High Court of Justice as having passed an Examination in pursuance of the said section; and such applicants may apply to Convocation to be allowed to pass such Examination before applying to the Court to be admitted as Solicitors; and the fees payable by such applicants shall be the same as those payable by applicants for Certificates of Fitness who come up in the ordinary way.

HONOURS, SCHOLARSHIPS, AND MEDALS.

The rules regulating Honors, Scholarships, and Medals, shall be as follows :

196. The Candidates who obtain at least three-fourths of the marks obtainable on the papers at either of the Intermediate Examinations, and at least one-third of the marks obtainable on the paper on each subject, shall be entitled to present themselves for a further examination for Honors and Scholarships on the same subjects, embracing the same number of questions, with the same aggregate value of marks obtainable in each subject.

197. For each of the Honor and Scholarship Examinations, a paper of questions shall be prepared by each of the Examiners, and they shall so manage and regulate the other details of the Examinations as to secure the objects of the Examinations, and the obtaining of the best and truest tests of the qualifications of Candidates for the standing Honors or Scholarships to be awarded.

198. The Candidates obtaining at least three-fourths of the aggregate marks obtainable on the papers in both the

Pass and Honor Examinations, and at least one-half of the aggregate marks obtainable on the papers in each subject on both Examinations, shall be passed with Honors, and each Candidate so passed shall receive a diploma certifying to the fact.

199. Those only who are Students-at-Law or Articled Clerks in their regular years are to be entitled to be passed with Honors, unless, in any particular case, Convocation shall see fit to award them.

200. Whenever a candidate for honours in the intermediate examinations is both a Student-at-Law and an Articled Clerk, the first day of the Term on which he was admitted on the books of the Society, and not the date of his articles, shall be the time from which the commencement of his year or course of study shall be reckoned, for the purpose of the examination for honours.

201. Of the Candidates passed with Honors, at each intermediate Examination, the first shall be entitled to a Scholarship of $100, the second to a Scholarship of $60, and the third to a Scholarship of $40, and each Scholar shall receive a diploma certifying to the fact.

202. The persons who obtain at least three-fourths of the marks obtainable on the Papers at the Examination for Call, and at least one-third of the marks obtainable on the Paper on each subject, shall be entitled to present themselves for a further Examination for Honors in the same subjects, embracing the same number of questions, with the same aggregate value of marks obtainable in each subject.

203. The persons obtaining at least three-fourths of the aggregate number of marks obtainable on the Papers in both the Pass and the Honor Examinations for Call, and at least one-half of the aggregate marks obtainable on the Papers in each subject in both Examinations, shall be called with Honors, and the Diploma of each person so called shall certify to his Call with Honors.

204. Of the persons called with Honors the first three shall be entitled to Medals, on the following conditions :

> *The First :* if he has passed both Intermediate Examinations with Honors, to a Gold Medal, otherwise to a Silver Medal

7

The Second: if he has passed both Intermediate Examinations with Honors, to a Silver Medal, otherwise to a Bronze Medal:

The Third: if he has passed both Intermediate Examinations with Honors, to a Bronze Medal.

205. The Diploma of each Medallist shall certify to his being such Medallist.

CALL OF BARRISTERS IN SPECIAL CASES.

206. The following persons may, as special cases, be called to practise at the Bar in Ontario

(1) Any person who has been duly admitted and enrolled, and has been in actual practice as a Solicitor of the Supreme Court of Judicature for Ontario, or an Attorney or Solicitor in the Superior Courts of any of the other Provinces of the Dominion, in which the same privilege is extended to Solicitors of the Supreme Court of Judicature for Ontario.

(2) Any person who has been duly called to the Bar of England, Scotland, or Ireland (excluding the Bar of merely local jurisdiction), when the Inn of Court or other authority having power to call or admit to the Bar, by which such person was called or admitted, extends the same privilege to Barristers from Ontario, on producing sufficient evidence of such call or admission, and testimonials of good character and conduct to the satisfaction of the Law Society.

(3) Any person who has been duly called to the Bar of the Superior Courts of any of the other Provinces of the Dominion in which the same privilege is extended to Barristers of Ontario.

207. Every such person, before being called to the Bar, shall furnish proof:

(1) That notice of his intention to apply for Call to the Bar was given during the term next preceding that in which he presents himself for Call, and was also published for at least two months preceding such last mentioned term, in the *Ontario Gazette.*

(2) That he was duly admitted and enrolled, and has been in actual practice, as an Attorney or Solicitor, as

mentioned in sub-section 1 of Rule 206; and that he still remains duly enrolled as such, and in good standing; and that since his admission as aforesaid no adverse application has been made to any Court or Courts to strike him off the Roll of any Court, or otherwise to disqualify him from practice as such Attorney or Solicitor, and that no charge is pending against him for professional or other misconduct.

(3) Or that he was duly called to and is still a member in good standing of the Bar, as mentioned in Sub-sections 2 and 3 of Rule 206, and that since his Call no adverse application has been made to disbar or otherwise disqualify him from practice at the Bar of which he claims to be a member, and that no charge is pending against him for professional or other misconduct.

(4) That he has passed the Examination hereinafter prescribed.

208. An Attorney or Solicitor on the Rolls of any of the Courts mentioned in the said Sub-section 1 of Rule 206 shall be examined with the ordinary Candidates for Call in the subjects prescribed for the Final Examination.

209. A Barrister as mentioned in Sub-sections 2 and 3 of Rule 206, shall pass such Examination as may be prescribed at the time of his application.

210. The fees payable by such Candidates for Call to the Bar in addition to the ordinary fees payable for Admission and for Call, shall be the sum of two hundred dollars.

ADMISSION OF SOLICITORS IN SPECIAL CASES.

211. The following persons may, as special cases, be admitted and enrolled as Solicitors of the Supreme Court of Judicature for Ontario :

(1) Any person who has been duly called to practice at the Bar of Ontario, or in any of the Superior Courts not having merely local jurisdiction, in England, Ireland, or Scotland, or in the Superior Courts in any of the other Provinces of the Dominion.

(2) Any person who has been duly admitted and enrolled as a Solicitor of the Supreme Court of Judicature in England, or as a Solicitor of the Court of Judicature in Ire-

land, or as a Writer to the Signet or a Solicitor in the Superior Courts of Scotland, or as an Attorney or Solicitor of any of Her Majesty's Superior Courts of Law or Equity in any of Her Majesty's Colonies, wherein the Common Law of England is the Common Law of the land.

212. Every such person before being admitted to practise as a Solicitor, shall, after complying with the provisions of Revised Statutes of Ontario, chapter 147, section 8, furnish proof :

(1) A Barrister as mentioned in Sub-section 1 of Rule 211, that he was bound by a contract in writing to a practising Solicitor in Ontario to serve, and has served him as his Articled Clerk for the period of three years.

(2) An Attorney, Solicitor, or Writer as mentioned in sub-section 2 of Rule 211, that he was bound by a contract in writing to a practising Solicitor in Ontario to serve, and has served him as his Articled Clerk for the period of.one year.

(3) That he has passed the usual examination in the subjects prescribed for the examination of Candidates for Certificate of Fitness to practise as Solicitor of the Supreme Court of Judicature for Ontario. .

(4) That notice of his intention to apply for admission as such Solicitor, was given during the Term next preceding that in which he presents himself for Examination and admission, and was also published for at least two months preceding such last mentioned Term in the *Ontario Gazette.*

213. The fees payable by such Candidates for admission to practise, in addition to the ordinary fees for articled clerks and for admission, shall be the sum of two hundred dollars.

ANNUAL FEES AND CERTIFICATES.

214. Every member of the Society shall, after his Call to the Bar, pay to the Society, through its Sub-Treasurer, a Term fee of $2 per annum, payable during Michaelmas Term in each year.

215. In case any Solicitor of the Supreme Court for Ontario, desirous of obtaining his Annual Certificate, according to the provisions of the Statute in that behalf,

pays on any day within the Term of Michaelmas, in any year, to the Sub-Treasurer of this Society, the sums hereinafter mentioned, according to the scale set forth in the Schedule hereunto annexed, together with all such other fees and dues, if any, as by the said Statute are required to be paid by him on obtaining such Annual Certificate, such Solicitor shall be thereupon entitled to such Certificate for the year commencing with the first day of such Michaelmas Term; and such Certificate shall be thereupon issued to him by the Secretary of the Society, as provided by the said Statute.

For a Certificate for all the Divisions of
the High Court of Justice.......... $15 00

For a Certificate for any of the said Divisions separately................. 15 00

The sum of fifteen dollars payable by each Solicitor for his Annual Certificate, shall not include the fee of two dollars per annum payable by each Barrister under Rule 214.

216. A list shall be delivered by the Secretary to the Publishers of the Reports immediately after the first day of January, yearly, of all those Solicitors who have taken out their Annual Certificates up to that date.

217. The fines for not taking out Certificates in due time, shall be as follows :—If such Certificate be not taken out before the first day of Hilary Term, in addition to the usual fee for Certificate, the further sum of two dollars for each Division of the High Court of Justice. If not taken out before the first day of Easter Term, the further sum of three dollars for each such Division of the High Court of Justice, in addition to the usual fee for Certificate ; and if not taken out before the first day of Trinity Term, the sum of four dollars for each such Division of the High Court of Justice, in addition to the usual fee for Certificate.

218. A record shall be kept by the Secretary of unpaid Certificates and Term Fees, with a view to the easy ascertainment of the amount of default.

219. A fee of two dollars shall be paid to the Secretary of the Society for the use of the Society on the presentation of every petition to the Benchers for special relief respecting fines or fees.

RESUMÉ OF FEES.

220. Every Candidate shall pay with his Notice
for Admission as Student-at-Law ....$ 1 00
And previous to his Admission 50 00

(*a*) Unless he shall have within the preceding five years
been admitted as Articled Clerk, in which case he shall
pay, instead of fifty dollars, the sum of ten dollars.

221. Every Candidate for Admission as Articled
Clerk, with his Notice shall pay 1 00
And previous to his Admission........... 40 00

222. Every Candidate with Notice of Call to the
Degree of Barrister-at-Law, shall pay...... 1 00
And previous to his Examination..........100 00
Additional Fee in Special Cases under
Statute 200 00

223. Every Candidate for Certificate of Fitness,
shall, on leaving Articles, pay............ 60 00
Additional Fee in Special Cases under
Statute 200 00

224. On every petition to Convocation for special
relief 2 00

225. For every Certificate of Admission as Student-at-Law or Articled Clerk, if required 1 00

226. For every Barrister's Diploma, if required. 2 00

227. And for every other Certificate, not by these
rules otherwise provided for 1 00

228. Law School, per Term, in advance 10 00

229. Barrister's Term fee, per annum.......... 2 00

230. Solicitor's Annual Certificate 15 00

231. In case any Candidate for admission on the books
as a Student or Articled Clerk, or for Call to the Bar, or
for a Certificate of Fitness as Solicitor, fails to pass the
necessary Examination, or is rejected on any other ground,
the fee required to be deposited by him for the use of the
Society according to the Statute or the Rules of the Society, shall be returned to him by the Treasurer, less $10.

APPENDIX.

A.

TREASURER'S SUMMONS FOR A SPECIAL CONVOCATION.

LAW SOCIETY OF UPPER CANADA, OSGOODE HALL, TO WIT :

    day, the   day of November, in   Term,
in the   year of the reign of Queen Victoria, A.D.
18 .

GENTLEMEN,—By virtue of the authority vested in me, as Treasurer of this Society, by the Rules thereof, I have thought fit to summon, and do hereby accordingly summon, A CONVOCATION OF THE BENCHERS OF THIS SO-CIETY, to be held in the Covocation-Chamber in Osgoode Hall, at the hour of ten o'clock in the forenoon of , the   day of , in this present Term.

This, therefore, is to notify you, and every of you of the same, pursuant to the Rules above mentioned, and to request your attendance, and the attendance of each of you, at the time and place aforesaid.

Yours, &c.

J. R.,
Treasurer.

To the Benchers of the Law }
Society of Upper Canada, and }
every of them. }

B.

NOTICE OF PRESENTATION.

LAW SOCIETY OF UPPER CANADA, OSGOODE HALL, TO WIT :

Mr. A. B. (some Bencher) gives notice that C. D. (names in full, no initials), of E., in the county of F., in this Province, Gentleman, son of G. D., of the same place, Merchant (or as the case may be), will next Term be presented to the Benchers of this Society in Convocation, for the purpose of being entered and admitted as a Student-at-Law (or Articled Clerk as the case may be.)

C.

PRESENTATION FOR ADMISSION.

LAW SOCIETY OF UPPER CANADA, OSGOODE HALL, TO WIT :

To the Benchers of the Law Society of Upper Canada in Convocation.

GENTLEMEN : I hereby present to the Committee and to Convocation, C. D., (names in full, no initials,) of E. in the County of F. in this Province, Gentleman, son of G. D., of the same place, Merchant, (or as the case may be) for the purpose of his being entered and admitted as a Student-at-Law, (or Articled Clerk, as the case may be.)

I. J.

(Some member of the Society of the degree of Barrister-at-Law).

D.

PETITION FOR ADMISSION.

LAW SOCIETY OF UPPER CANADA, OSGOODE HALL, TO WIT :

To the Benchers of the Law Society of Upper Canada, in Convocation.

The Petition of C D., (Christian and surname at length, no initials) of E. in the County of F. in this Province, Gentleman, son of G. D., of the same place, Merchant, (or as the case may be,) most respectfully sheweth : That your Petitioner is of the full age of —— years ; that he has received an education which he trusts sufficiently qualifies him to commence the study of the profession of the Law ; that he received his education at the University of Oxford ; (or at Upper Canada College, Upper Canada Academy, or at the school of G. A., at Z., in the County of F., in this Province, or as the case may be, being as full and particular as possible) ; that in the course of such instruction he has read the following books, that is to say, (as the case may be) ; that your Petitioner is desirous of becoming a member of the Law Society of Upper Canada, and of being entered thereof as a Student-at-Law, (or Articled Clerk, as the case may be.)

Your Petitioner therefore, most respectfully prays that his qualifications being first examined and found sufficient, according to the Rules of the Society, and Standing orders of Convocatiom in that behalf, he may be admitted and entered accordingly ; and he doth hereby undertake and promise that he will, well, faithfully, and truly submit, and conform himself to, and obey, observe, perform, fulfil, and keep all the Rules, Resolutions, Orders, and Regulations of the Society, during such time as he shall continue on the books of the said Society, as a member thereof.

Witness,   C. D.

    R. W.   Term, 18 Vic.

E.

CERTIFICATE OF ADMISSION INTO THE SOCIETY.

LAW SOCIETY OF UPPER CANADA, OSGOODE HALL, TO WIT :

These are to certify that C. D., of E., in the County of F., Merchant, (or as the case may be,) having complied with the Rules in that behalf and been classed in the Graduate (or Matriculant, as the case may be) Class, was by the Benchers of the Law Society of Upper Canada in Convocation, on the   day of   in the Term of   in the year of our Lord one thousand eight hundred and duly admitted into the said Society as a member thereof, and entered as a Student-at-Law, (or Articled Clerk, as the case may be), taking precedence as such in this Society next immediately after Mr. Y. R., and that he now remains on the books of the Society as a member thereof.

In testimony whereof, I, J. R., Treasurer of the said Society, have to these presents affixed the seal of the said Society at Osgoode Hall, this   day of   in the year of our Lord one thousand eight hundred and   and in the   year of her Majesty's reign.

J. M. C., *Secretary.*   J. R., *Treasurer.*

F.

NOTICE OF PRESENTATION FOR CALL.

LAW SOCIETY OF UPPER CANADA, OSGOODE HALL, TO WIT :

Mr. A. B. (some Bencher) gives notice that C. D., (names in full) a Member of this Society, now standing on the books as a Student-at-Law, and who has received his professional education under L. J., Esq., one of the Members of this Society, of the Degree of Barrister-at-Law, (or of I. J. K., L. M. N., members of this Society, of the Degree of Barrister-at-Law, as the case may be) will, next Term, be presented to the Benchers of this Society in Convocation, for the purpose of being called to the Bar.

8

58

G.

PRESENTATION FOR CALL.

LAW SOCIETY OP UPPER CANADA, OSGOODE HALL, TO WIT:

To the Benchers of the Law Society of Upper Canada in Convocation.

GENTLEMEN,—I hereby present to the Convocation C. D., (names in full) a Member of this Society, now standing on the books as a Student-at-Law, and who has received his professional education under my superintendence, (or under the superintendence of K. L. M. N. O., Esqrs., Members of this Society, of the Degree of Barrister-at-Law,) for the purpose of his being called to the Degree of Barrister-at-Law.

I. J.

(Some Member of the Society of the Degree of Barrister-at-Law.)

H.

BOND.

LAW SOCIETY OF UPPER CANADA, OSGOODE HALL, TO WIT:

Know all men by these presents, that we C. D., (names in full) of E., in the county of F., in this Province Gentleman, Member of the Law Society of Upper Canada, now standing on the books of the said Law Society as a Student-at-Law (or Esquire, Member of the Honorable Society of Lincoln's Inn, Gray's Inn, the Middle Temple, or the Inner Temple, as the case may be, duly called to practise at the Bar of Her Majesty's Superior Courts in England, or Esquire, duly called to practice at the Bar in Her Majesty's Province of Quebec, Nova Scotia, or New Brunswick, &c., as the case may be), and Z. D. of E. in the county of F., merchant, and V N. of T. in the County of S., yeoman, are jointly and severally held and firmly bound to the Law Society of Upper Canada in the penal sum of Four Hundred Dollars of lawful money of Canada to be paid to the Law Society of Upper Canada aforesaid; for which payment to be well and truly made we bind ourselves, and each of us binds himself, our and each and every of our heirs, executors and administrators firmly by these presents. Sealed with our Seals. Dated this day of   , in the   year of Her Majesty's reign, and in the year one thousand eight hundred and

The condition of this obligation is such that if the above
bounden C. D. (names in full) shall and will well and truly
pay, or cause to be paid, to the Law Society of Upper
Canada aforesaid, all such fees and dues of what nature or
kind soever, as now are due or payable by or from him to
the said Society, by or under any Statute or by any Rule,
Resolution, Order, or Regulation of the said Society, passed by
the said Society, or by the Benchers thereof, with the approbation
of the Judges of the Province, as Visitors of the said Society, or
which shall or may hereafter become due or payable by or for
him to the said Society, under the same or under any other
Statute or by the same or any other Rule, Resolution, Order, or
Regulation passed or to be passed by the Benchers of the said
Society in Convocation, with such approbation as aforesaid ; and
also do and shall moreover, well, faithfully and truly obey, observe, perform, fulfil and keep all the Rules, Resolutions, Orders,
and Regulations of the said Society, passed as aforesaid, and now
in force, or hereafter to be passed, as aforesaid, during such time
as he shall continue on the books of the said Society as a member
thereof—then this obligation shall be void, otherwise the same
shall be and remain in full force, virtue, and effect.

Sealed and delivered in the presence of
A.B.

L.S.
L.S.
L.S.

I.

CERTIFICATE ON BOND.

LAW SOCIETY OF UPPER CANADA, OSGOODE HALL, TO WIT :

These are to certify that we, the subscribers hereunto, are
well acquainted with the within named Z. D. and V. N., and
that they are freeholders of substance amply sufficient to secure
the performance of the condition of the within bond.

J. S.
J. R.

J.

PETITION FOR CALL.

To the Benchers of the Law Society of Upper Canada, in Convocation.

The Petition of C.D. (Christian and surnames at length, no initials,) of E., in the County of F., in this Province, Gentleman, son of G. D., of the same place, Merchant, (or as the case may be), and a member of this Society, now standing on the books as a Student-at-Law most respectfully sheweth,—That your Petitioner is of the full age of   years ; that he has received a professional education which he trusts sufficiently qualifies him to commence the practice of the Profession of the Laws : that he is of   years' standing on the books of the Society as a Student-at-Law ; and that he has received his professional education under the superintendence of J. K. (or of J. K. for the space of two years, L. M. for one year, and N. O. for two years, or as the case may be) a member of this Society of the Degree of Barrister-at-Law ; that he has since his admission into the Society, passed the first and second Intermediate Examinations in the Term of   18   and of   18 respectively.

That he has since his admission into the Society pursued the following branches of general learning that is to say, (as the case may be.)

That in the course of such pursuit he has read the following works, that is to say, (as the case may be.)

That he has particularly studied the following branches of the law, that is to say, (as the case may be.)

That in the course of such study he has read the following works, that is to say, (as the case may be.)

That he is under no articles of Clerkship of any kind whatsoever to any person or persons (or as the case may be) ; and that he is desirous of being called to the Degree of Barrister-at-Law.

Your Petitioner, therefore, most respectfully prays, that his qualifications being first examined and found sufficient according to the Rules of the Society, and the Standing Orders of Convocation in that behalf, he may be called to the said Degree accordingly; and he doth hereby undertake and promise that he will, faithfully and truly, submit and conform himself to, obey, observe, perform, fulfil and keep all the Rules, Resolutions, Orders, and Regulations of the said Society, during such time as he shall continue on the books of the said Society as a member thereof.

Witness,   C. D.
N. P.   Michaelmas Term   Vic.

K.

DIPLOMA OF BARRISTER AT LAW.

LAW SOCIETY OF UPPER CANADA, OSGOODE HALL, TO WIT :

Be it remembered that C. D. of E. in the county of F., in this Province, Gentleman, son of G. D., of the same place, Merchant (or, as the case may be,) was by the Benchers of the Law Society of Upper Canada in Convocation, on   the day of   of the Term of   in the year of our Lord one thousand eight hundred and   , duly called to the Degree of Barrister-at-Law, and that he now remains on the books of this Society as a Barrister thereof.

In testimony whereof, I, J. R., Treasurer of the said Society, have to these presents affixed the Seal of the said Society, at Osgoode Hall, this   day of   in the year of our Lord one thousand eight hundred and   and in the   year of Her Majesty's reign.

J. M. C., *Secretary.*   J. R., *Treasurer.*

L.

PETITION FOR CERTIFICATE OF FITNESS.

LAW SOCIETY OF UPPER CANADA, OSGOODE HALL, TO WIT :

To the Benchers of the Law Society of Upper Canada, in Convocation.

The Petition of   most respectfully sheweth—
That your Petitioner is of the full age of   years ; That he has received a professional education, which he trusts sufficiently qualifies him to commence the Practice of the Profession of the Law ; That he received his professional education under the superintendence of   an Attorney of Her Majesty's Courts of Queen's Bench and Common Pleas and a Solicitor of the Court of Chancery and of the Supreme Court for Ontario ; That he was admitted into the Law Society as a Member thereof, and entered on the Books thereof as a Student of the Laws in the Term of   18   ; That the degree of B.A. was conferred on him on   day of   18   , by the University of   ; That his Articles of Clerkship were dated and executed on the   day of   18   and were duly filed on the   day of   18   ; That he passed the Intermediate Examinations as follows :

1st Intermediate Examination in   Term 18
2nd   "   "   in   "   18

That he has particularly studied the following branches of the Law, that is to say : Those mentioned in the Law Society Curriculum ; That in the course of such study he has read the following works, that is to say : Those mentioned in the Law Society Curriculum ; That his Articles of Clerkship expire on the day of   18 , and that he is desirous of receiving a Certificate of Fitness and of being admitted as an Attorney and Solicitor.

Your Petitioner, therefore, most respectfully prays that his qualifications, being first examined and found sufficient according to the Rules of the Society, and Standing Orders of Convocation in that behalf, he may receive a Certificate of Fitness accordingly.

Witness,   Term, 18

M.

ARTICLES OF CLERKSHIP.

ARTICLES OF AGREEMENT made the   day of   in the year of our Lord 18 , between A. A., of   , gentleman, (the father or guardian) of the first part, B. A. (the clerk) (son of the said A. A.) of the second part, and S. S. (the Solicitor), of   , gentleman, one of the Solicitors of the Supreme Court of Judicature, of the third part.

WITNESS, that the said B. A. of his own free will, (and with the consent and approbation of the said A. A., testified by his execution of these presents,) hath placed and bound himself, and by these presents doth place and bind himself, clerk to the said S. S., to serve him from the day of the date hereof up to the day on which he shall be admitted as a Student-at-Law or entered as an Articled Clerk, whichever shall first happen in accordance with the rules of the Law Society, and during and until the full end and term of   years from the day of his so being admitted or entered then next ensuing :

And the said A. A. doth hereby for himself, his heirs, executors, and administrators, covenant with the said S. S., his executors, administrators, and assigns, that the said B. A. shall and will well, faithfully and diligently serve the said S. S. as his clerk in the practice or profession of a Solicitor of the Supreme Court from the date hereof, during and until the full end of the hereinbefore mentioned term ; And that the said B. A. shall not, at any time during such term, cancel, obliterate, injure, spoil, destroy, waste, embezzel, spend, or make away with any of the books, papers, writings, documents, moneys, stamps, chattels, or other property of the said S. S., his executors, administrators, or assigns, or of his partner or partners, or of any of his clients or employers :

And that in case the said B. A. shall act contrary to the last-mentioned covenant, or if the said S. S., his executors, administrators, or assigns, or his partner or partners, shall sustain or suffer any loss or damage by the misbehaviour, neglect, or improper conduct of the said B. A. the said A. A., his heirs, executors, or administrators, shall indemnify the said S. S., and make good and reimburse him the amount or value thereof: And further, that the said B. A. will at all times keep the secrets of the said S. S and his partner or partners, and will at all times during said term readily and cheerfully obey and execute his or their lawful and reasonable commands ; and shall not depart or absent himself from the service or employ of the said S. S. at any time during the said term without his consent first obtained, and shall from time to time, and at all times during the said term, conduct himself with all due diligence, honesty, and propriety : And the said B. A. doth hereby covenant with the said S. S., his executors, administrators, and assigns, that he, the said B. A., will truly, honestly, and diligently serve the said S. S. at all times during the said term, as a faithful clerk ought to do, in all things whatsoever, in the manner above specified.

In consideration whereof and of   paid by the said A. A. the receipt whereof the said S. S. doth hereby acknowledge) the said S. S. for himself, his heirs, executors, and administrators, doth hereby covenant with the said B. A., that the said S. S. will accept and take the said B. A. as his clerk : And also, that the said S. S. will by the best ways and means he may or can, and to the utmost of his skill or knowledge, teach and instruct, or cause to be taught or instructed, the said B. A., in the said practice or profession of a Solicitor of the Supreme Court, which the said S. S. now doth, or shall at any time hereafter during the said term use or practice : And also will, at the expiration of the said term use his best means and endeavours, at the request, costs, and charges of the said A. A. and B. A. or either of them, to cause and procure him the said B. A. to be admitted as a solicitor of the Supreme Court, provided the said B. A. shall have well, faithfully, and diligently served his said intended clerkship:

In witness whereof the parties to these presents have hereunto set their hands and seals, the day and year first above mentioned.

Signed, sealed, and delivered by the ⎫   A. A.   (L.S.)
within named parties, in the presence ⎬   B. A.   (L.S.)
of   W. F.   ⎭   S. S.   (L.S.)

Note.—Where the person about to be articled has attained his majority his father or guardian is not a necessary party to the instrument.

County of } I.
　　　　　　of the　　　　　　　　　of
　　　　　　in the Connty of
　　To Wit: }　　　　　　　　　make oath and say ;

1. THAT I was personally present, and did see the within Instrument and Duplicate thereof duly signed, sealed and executed by

　　　　　　　　　　　　the part　　thereto :

2. THAT the said Instrument and Duplicate were executed at

3. THAT I know the said part

4. THAT I am a subscribing witness to the said Instrument and Duplicate.

5. THAT the said instrument and Duplicate were executed as aforesaid on the　　　　　day of　　　　　18

SWORN before me, at
in the County of
this　　　　day of
in the year of our Lord 18 }

　　A Commissioner for taking affidavits in H. C. J., etc.

DEED OF SURRENDER.

THE LAW SOCIETY TO HER MAJESTY.

Approved,

(Signed.)   J. G. SCOTT.

THIS INDENTURE made the First day of July, in the year of our Lord, One Thousand Eight Hundred and Seventy-four.

BETWEEN the Law Society of Upper Canada of the First Part

AND Her Majesty the Queen of the Second Part : WITNESSETH, WHEREAS the Legislative Assembly of the Province of Ontario at its last Session passed a resolution approving of the cancellation by His Excellency, the Lieutenant-Governor of the Province of Ontario, if he should see fit, of the existing agreement dated the Twentieth day of June, in the year of our Lord, One Thousand Eight Hundred and Forty-six, BETWEEN the Law Society of Upper Canada and the Government of the late Province of Canada, which resolution is as follows : "That this House approves of the cancellation by His Excellency the Lieutenant-Governor, if he shall see fit, of the existing agreement dated 20th June, 1846, between the Law Society of Upper Canada and the Government of the late Province of Canada, such cancellation to be on the condition that the said Society surrender to Her Majesty the buildings and lands belonging to the said Society, now used for the accommodation of the Superior Courts, namely, the Centre part and the West Wing of the building in the City of Toronto, known as Osgoode Hall, with the land upon which the said building stands, the land North and West of the said Centre building and West Wing, and the roadway South of the said land, and on further condition that no building or erection be put up on the land retained by the said Society, and forming part of the Osgoode Hall property, except for the use or occupation of the said Society, and that no building or erection be put up for the use or occupation of the said Society without first obtaining the approval of the Lieutenant-Governor in Council, due provision to be made for securing all rights of way or passage which the Lieutenant-Governor shall deem necessary or proper the land so surrendered by the said Society not to be built upon, except for purposes connected with the Superior Courts and the offices relating thereto. The Law Society to have the control of the rooms known as the Library and the Benchers, Barristers and Secretary's rooms. The Society to enter into covenants for keeping the grounds connected with Osgoode Hall in proper order and condition at the expense of the Society, and the cancellation to be subject to such other terms and conditions as His Excellency shall deem proper for carrying out of the said objects.

AND WHEREAS, these presents are executed, made, and delivered and entered into, accepted, received and taken as a compliance with, and a full performance of the conditions in said resolution.

Now THIS INDENTURE, WITNESSETH, that the said Law Society of Upper Canada, grant, surrender and yield up unto Her Majesty the Queen and her successors.

ALL AND SINGULAR, that certain piece or parcel of land, being part of the front or south part of park lot number eleven in the first concession from the bay formerly in the Township of York now in the City of Toronto, better known and described as follows, that is to say : Commencing at a point on the South side of Osgoode Street, in said City of Toronto, where the East side of University Street intersects the same; thence Easterly along the Southerly limit of Osgoode Street, a distance of three hundred and fifty-one feet and four inches ; thence Southerly in a line parallel with University Street, two hundred and fifty-eight feet and two inches ; thence Easterly on a line parallel with Osgoode Street, twenty-three feet and five inches ; thence Southerly on a line parallel with University

9

Street, twenty-two feet two inches ; thence Westerly on a line parallel with Osgoode Street, thirty-one feet ; thence Southerly on a line parallel with University Street, eighty-two feet and three inches ; thence Westerly on a line parallel with Osgoode Street, three hundred and forty-two feet and eight inches, more or less, to a point on the East side of University Street ; thence Northerly along the East limit of University Street to the place of beginning, together with the building erected thereon, the said lands, premises and buildings hereinbefore particularly described by metes and bounds, being known as the buildings and lands belonging to the said Society, and at the time of passing of the said resolution, and now used for the occupation accommodation of the Superior Courts, namely, the Centre part and the West Wing of the building, in the City of Toronto, known as Osgoode Hall, with the lands on which the said Centre building and West Wing and the roadway south of the said land, subject, however, to the reservation by the said Law Society of the free and exclusive use by them of the rooms in the said building, now commonly known as the Library, the room off the Northwest corner of the Library, commonly known as the Librarian's room, otherwise called the Secretary's room, and the free and unrestricted right of ingress, egress and regress to, in and from such Library, Benchers and Librarian's rooms as now used and enjoyed, and subject to the further reservation to the said Society and their successors from time to time, and at all times forever hereafter to have the free use and enjoyment of the said ways approaching to such buildings, and to go, return, pass and repass with horses, waggons and other carriages laden or unladen, on, through, along and over said roadways at all times hereafter.

AND the said Law Society of Upper Canada do hereby for themselves and their successors covenant, promise and agree with Her Majesty the Queen, her heirs and successors in manner following, that is to say :

"That the said Law Society and their successors will from time to time, and at all times hereafter, and at their own costs and expenses, repair and amend, and keep repaired and amended in a proper, substantial and workmanlike manner all the roads, ways and foot paths in the block of land commonly known as the Osgoode Hall block, a parcel whereof is hereby granted and surrendered, and the gates by which such roads, ways or foot paths are entered, and the locks and fastenings thereto belonging, whither the same are upon the land hereby granted or upon the portion of the block retained, and that the public shall, at all proper times and seasons, have access to such buildings before mentioned, and for such purpose to go, return, pass and repass over such roads, ways or foot paths as are upon the said portion of the said block retained as aforesaid, and through such gates upon such last mentioned portion at all times hereafter, forever, and shall also have the like liberty to go, return, pass and repass over such roads, ways and foot paths as are or may be made upon the portion hereby surrendered, and through the gates that are or may be thereon, as long as the same are left under the control or care of the said Law Society.

And that the said Law Society will from time to time, and at all times hereafter, at the like costs and expenses of the said Society and their successors, repair and renew, and keep repaired and renewed, and put and keep in order the trees and shrubbery and grass upon said Osgoode Hall block, so that the same shall continue in as ornamental a condition as they now are. And will not erect, or cause to be erected, or allow to be erected on the said residue of the said land and premises, or portions of the said Osgoode Hall block, retained by the said Society as aforesaid, any building or buildings, except such as may be required for the purposes and accommodations of said Law Society ; nor shall erect, or attempt or commence to erect, any such building or buildings without first obtaining therefore the approval of the Lieutenant-Governor of the Province of Ontario in Council.

And the said Law Society grants unto Her Majesty, her heirs and successors forever, hereafter the free use and enjoyment in common with the said Society of the coal bins and yard room now used in connection with the engine room of the said Society, for the purpose of storing wood and coal, and ingress and egress thereto.

IN WITNESS whereof, the parties hereto have affixed their respective Seals, namely, the Great Seal of the Province of Ontario and the Seal of the Law Society of Upper Canada, the day and year first written.

WITNESS:
"FRANK J. MADILL." }

"J. HILLYARD CAMERON,"
Treasurer. [L.S.]

DEED BETWEEN THE QUEEN AND THE LAW SOCIETY OF UPPER CANADA.

I certify that the within instrument is duly entered and registered in the Registry Office for the City of Toronto in Book 26 for Centre West Toronto, at 2.55 o'clock p.m. of the 26th day of February, A.D. 1886.

(Signed.)   WM. BENNETT,
Deputy Registrar.

PROVINCE OF ONTARIO.   [SEAL].

(Signed)   OLIVER MOWAT,
Attorney-General.

(Signed)   JOHN BEVERLEY ROBINSON.

THIS INDENTURE made this 26th day of November, in the year of our Lord, One Thousand Eight Hundred and Eighty-five.

BETWEEN

THE LAW SOCIETY OF UPPER CANADA, of the first part,
And

HER MAJESTY THE QUEEN of the second part.

WHEREAS under and by virtue of a certain Deed of Surrender dated on the First day of July, in the year of our Lord, One Thousand Eight Hundred and Seventy-four, made between the said Law Society of Upper Canada of the first part, and Her Majesty the Queen of the second part, the said Law Society of Upper Canada did grant, surrender, and yield up unto Her Majesty the Queen and her successors certain portions of grounds and buildings known as the Centre Part and West Wing of the buildings in the City of Toronto, known as Osgoode Hall, with the land upon which the said building then stood and now stands, and the land North and West of the said Centre building and West Wing and the roadway South of the said land described by metes and bounds as therein is set forth and contained,

AND WHEREAS since the execution of the said Deed of Surrender it has been ascertained that the boundary line which was thereby described between that portion of the said buildings and land thereby granted and surrendered to Her Majesty as aforesaid, and the portion which was retained or intended to be retained by the said Law Society, was inaccurately defined having regard to the intention of the parties to the said Deed and having regard to the position of said buildings upon the said lands.

AND WHEREAS a new Boiler House having been built it has also been agreed that the old Boiler House shall be granted to the Law Society, subject however, to the Agreement hereinafter contained in reference thereto.

AND WHEREAS it has been agreed that a Deed of Rectification and Confirmation shall be executed which shall convey to each of the said parties the several parts of the said Osgoode Hall buildings and grounds upon which it has been agreed by the parties should be granted and held by either party hereto (which said parts or portions may be conveniently explained or understood by reference to the plan or sketch hereunder drawn), and in order to rectify the inaccuracy of the description in the said before in part recited Deed and Surrender and these presents are executed in pursurance of the said Agreement.

Now THIS INDENTURE WITNESSETH that in consideration of the premises and of the sum of One Dollar paid to the said Law Society by the Treasurer of Ontario ; the said Law Society doth hereby grant, surrender, yield up, and confirm to Her Majesty and her successors.

ALL AND SINGULAR that certain parcel or tract of land and premises being composed of part of Park Lot Eleven, in the City of Toronto, and which may be more particularly known and described as follows, that is to say : Commencing where the South limit of Osgoode Street, in the said City of Toronto intersects the East limit of University Street, thence Easterly along the Southerly limit of Osgoode Street a distance of three hundred and fifty-three feet ten inches, thence Southerly parallel with University Street two hundred and fifty-four feet eleven inches to the North face of the wall of the old Boiler House, thence Westerly eight feet more or less to the face of the wall of the main building of Osgoode Hall, thence Southerly along the said face of the said wall twenty-two feet to the face of the Northerly wall of the old East Wing of Osgoode Hall, thence Westerly along the said face one foot one inch to the Northwest angle of the said East Wing, thence Southerly along the Westerly line of the wall of the East Wing four feet five inches to the face of the Southerly wall of the main building. thence Westerly and along the said face two feet six inches, thence Southerly parallel with University Street eighty-one feet three inches, thence Westerly parallel with Osgoode Street to University Street, thence Northerly along the Easterly limit of University Street to the place of beginning.

TOGETHER with the buildings erected thereon the said lands, premises and buildings hereinbefore particularly described by metes and bounds, being known as the buildings and lands belonging to the said Society, and at the time of passing of the Resolution hereinafter mentioned and now used for the accommodation of the Superior Courts, namely, the Centre Part and the West Wing of the building in the City of Toronto, known as Osgoode Hall with the land on which the said building stands the land North and West of the said Centre building and West Wing and the roadway South of the said land.

SUBJECT, however, to the reservation by the said Law Society of the free and exclusive use by them of the rooms in the said building now commonly known as the Library, the room off the Northwest corner of the Library commonly known as the Bencher's Room, the room off the Northeast corner of the Library commonly known as the Librarians' Room otherwise called the Secretary's Room, and the free and unrestricted right of ingress, egress and regress to in and from such Library, Bencher's, and Librarian's Rooms as now used and enjoyed.

AND SUBJECT to the further reservation to the said Society and their successors from time to time, and at all times forever hereafter to have the free use and enjoyment of the roadways approaching to such buildings and to go, return, pass and re-pass with horses, waggons, and other carriages, laden or unladen, on, through, along, and over said roadways at all times hereafter.

AND THIS INDENTURE FURTHER WITNESSETH that Her Majesty doth hereby grant and confirm to the said Law Society of Upper Canada and their successors the following lands, that is to say : Commencing on the South limit of Osgoode Street in the said City of Toronto at a point distant three hundred and fifty-three feet ten inches measured Easterly

69

from the East limit of University Street, thence Southerly parallel with University Street two hundred and fifty-four feet eleven inches to the North face of the wall of the old Boiler House, thence Westerly eight feet more or less to face of wall of main building of Osgoode Hall, thence Southerly along the said face of the said wall twenty-two feet to the face of the Northerly wall of the old East wing of Osgoode Hall, thence Westerly along the said wall one foot one inch to the Northwest angle of the said East Wing, thence Southerly along the Westerly line of the wall of the East Wing four feet five inches to the face of the Southerly wall of the main building, thence Westerly along the said Southerly face two feet six inches, thence Southerly parallel with University Street eighty-one feet three inches, thence Westerly parallel with Osgoode Street to the East side of University Street, thence Southerly along the East side of University Street to the North side of Queen Street, thence Easterly along the North side of Queen Street to the West side of Chestnut Street, thence Northerly along west side of Chestnut Street to the South side of Osgoode Street, thence Westerly along the South side of Osgoode Street to the place of beginning together with all buildings thereon erected.

AND the said Law Society for itself, its successors, and assigns hereby covenants with Her Majesty and her successors that if at any time hereafter the said Boiler House is destroyed by fire that the said Society will convey to Her Majesty and her successors that part of the land on which the said Boiler House is built lying West of the continuation Southerly to the face of the Northerly wall of said East Wing of the line hereinbefore mentioned which may be more particularly described as follows that is to say : Commencing at a point on the North side of the old Boiler House where it is intersected by a line drawn Southerly through a point on the South limit of Osgoode Street parallel with University Street distant three hundred and fifty-three feet ten inches Easterly from the East limit of University Street, thence from the point of commencement still Southerly parallel with University Street fourteen feet six inches to the South side of said old Boiler House, thence Westerly along said South side of Boiler House eight feet to the East face of the East wall of the main building, thence Northerly along said East face fourteen feet six inches to the intersection of the North side of old Boiler House, thence Easterly along said side eight feet more or less to the place of beginning.

AND WHEREAS under an Agreement dated on or about the Twentieth day of June, One Thousand Eight Hundred and Forty-six, between the said Law Society of Upper Canada and the Government of the late Province of Canada ; the said Law Society did covenant to find and provide accommodation for the Superior Courts of Law and Equity.

AND WHEREAS the Cancellation of the said Covenant was approved by a Resolution of the Legislative Assembly of the Province of Ontario passed in the Session of the said Assembly held in the year One Thousand Eight Hundred and Seventy-three.

NOW THIS INDENTURE FURTHER WITNESSETH that for good and valuable considerations fully satisfied, Her Majesty the Queen doth release the Law Society of Upper Canada from the performance or observance of the said Covenant and from every obligation therein contained and from all liability thereunder whether in the past, in the present, or in the future.

IN WITNESS WHEREOF the parties to these presents have affixed their Seals, namely, the Great Seal of the Province of Ontario, and the Seal of the Law Society of Upper Canada the day and year first above writen.

(Signed) EDWARD BLAKE,
Treasurer.

(Signed) J. H. ESTEN,
Secretary, L. S.

Law Society Seal.
J. H. E.

Osgoode Street.

< 335 ft. 10 in. > ∧

Property of
Ontario Government.

254 ft. 11 in.

Law Society,

8 ft. ∨

Main Building.

Boiler House.

22 ft.

University Street.

Chestnut Street.

Gravel road.

81 ft. 3 in.

2 | 4.5

2.6'

1 ft. 1 in. +

Property of

Property of Law Society.

Queen Street.

York St.

By Command,
(Signed) ARTHUR S. HARDY,
Provincial Secretary.

An Act respecting the Law Society of Upper Canada.

[Rev. Stat. Ont. 1887, Chap. 145.]

HER MAJESTY, by and with the advice and consent of the Legislative Assembly of the Province of Ontario, enacts as follows:

LAW SOCIETY CONTINUED.

1. The Law Society of Upper Canada shall continue as at present constituted, subject to the provisions of this Act, and to the by-laws, resolutions, rules and regulations of the said Society in force at the time this Act takes effect, except so far as the same are inconsistent with this Act, until altered by the Benchers of said Society pursuant to this Act. R. S. O. 1877, c. 138, s. 1.

2. The Treasurer and Benchers of the said Society, heretofore incorporated, and their successors, shall continue to be a body corporate and politic, by the name of the Law Society of Upper Canada, and without license of mortmain may purchase, take, possess, and after acquiring the same, sell, lease or depart with any lands, tenements or hereditaments for the purposes of the said Society, but for no other purpose, and may execute all other matters pertaining to them to do. R. S. O. 1877, c. 138, s. 2.

VISITORS.

3. The Judges of the Supreme Court of Judicature shall be Visitors of the Society. R. S. O. 1877, c. 138, s. 3.

BENCHERS.

4. The Attorney-General of Canada for the time being and every person who has held that office, if a member of the Bar of Ontario, and the Attorney-General for the time being of Ontario, and all members of the Bar of Ontario, who have at any time held the office of Attorney-General of Ontario, or of Attorney-General or Solicitor-General for that part of the late Province of Canada, formerly called Upper Canada, and any retired Judge of the Supreme Court shall respectively, *ex-officio*, be Benchers of the Society. R. S. O. 1877, c. 138, s. 4.

5. The Benchers of the Law Society, exclusive of *ex-officio* members, shall be thirty in number, to be elected as hereinafter provided. R. S. O. 1877, c. 138, s. 5.

6.—(1) The Benchers shall, during the Term next preceding an election, appoint (with their assent) two persons, who, with the Treasurer, shall act as scrutineers at the election; and the said

Benchers shall also, during the said preceding Term, appoint a third person, who shall act for and as the Treasurer, in case he should be absent during the meeting of the scrutineers to count the votes. R. S. O. 1877, c. 138, s. 6.

(2) The first two mentioned scrutineers shall be members of the Law Society, but shall not be eligible for election to the office of Bencher, and their names shall be printed on the voting paper to be sent by the Secretary of the Society to each voter. 50 V. c. 8, Sched.

7. An election shall be held on the first Thursday after the first Wednesday in April, 1891, and the subsequent elections shall be held on the first Thursday after the first Wednesday in April of every fifth year thereafter; but in case the scrutineers are unable to complete the scrutiny upon such day, the same shall be continued from day to day until the election is declared. In case any scrutineer is absent during the scrutiny the others may nevertheless proceed therewith. R. S. O. 1877, c. 138, s. 7.

8. Each member of the Bar, not hereinafter declared ineligible as an elector, may vote for thirty persons. R. S. O. 1877, c. 138, s. 8.

9. The votes shall be given by closed voting papers, in the form in the Schedule to this Act, or to the like effect, being delivered to the Secretary of the Law Society on the first Wednesday of April of the year proper for the election, or during the Monday and Tuesday immediately preceding. Any voting papers received by the said Secretary by post during said days, or during the preceding week, shall be deemed delivered to him. R. S. O. 1877, c. 138, s. 9.

10. It shall be the duty of the Secretary to send to each member of the Bar whose name is on the alphabetical list or register mentioned in section 17, where his residence is known to the Secretary, one copy of the said form of voting paper applicable to the election then next to be held. Such form shall be sent in such manner and at such time before the holding of the election as may be directed by rule of the Benchers in convocation. 50 V. c. 8, Sched.

11. It shall be the duty of the Secretary to send with the said form of voting paper, a list of those persons then already Benchers of the Law Society ex-officio, and of those whose term of office is about to expire. 50 V. c. 8, Sched.

12. The said voting papers shall, upon the Thursday following, be opened by the Secretary of the Law Society in the presence of the scrutineers, who shall scrutinize and count the votes, and keep a record thereof in a proper book to be provided by the said Society. R. S. O. 1877, c. 138, s. 10.

13. The thirty persons who have the highest number of votes shall be Benchers of the said Law Society for the next term of five years. R. S. O. 1877, c. 138, s. 11.

14. Any person entitled to vote at such election shall be entitled to be present at the opening of the said voting papers. R. S. O. 1877, c. 138, s. 12.

15. In case of an equality of votes between two or more persons, which leaves the election of one or more Benchers undecided, then the said scrutineers shall forthwith put into a ballot-box a number

of papers, with the names of the candidates having such equality of votes written thereon, one for each candidate, and the Secretary of the Society shall draw by chance from the ballot-box, in the presence of the scrutineers, one or more of such papers sufficient to make up the required number, and the persons whose names are upon the papers so drawn shall be the Benchers. R. S. O. 1877, c. 138, s. 13.

16. No person shall be entitled to vote at an election unless all his bar fees to the Law Society have been paid. R. S. O. 1877, c. 138, s. 14.

17.—(1) The Secretary of the Law Society shall, on the first day of the Term previous to the time for any election, make out an alphabetical list or register of the members of the Bar who are entitled to vote at the succeeding election, and such register may be examined by any member of the said Society at all reasonable times, at the office of the said Secretary.

(2) In case any member of the Society complains to the Secretary, in writing, of the improper omission or insertion of any name in the list, it shall be the duty of the Secretary forthwith to examine into the complaint and rectify the error if any there be ; and in case any person is dissatisfied with the decision of the Secretary, he may appeal to the persons who have been appointed to act as scrutineers for the next election thereafter, and the decision of the scrutineers shall be final, and such list shall remain or be altered in accordance with their decision.

(3) The Secretary shall add to the list the names of all persons who have been called to the Bar during the Term previous to the election ; and no alteration shall be made to the list except as is provided in this section ; and the list, as it stands revised upon the last Monday of the said last-mentioned Term, shall be the register of persons entitled to vote at the next election.

(4) No person whose name is not inserted in the said list shall be entitled to vote at the election. R. S. O. 1877, c. 138, s. 15.

18. No person shall be eligible as a Bencher at any election, who is not qualified to vote at the election. R. S. O. 1877, c. 138, s. 16.

19. At all elections retiring Benchers shall be eligible for re-election. R. S. O. 1877, c. 138, s. 17.

20. Any votes cast for any person who is ineligible to be a Bencher, or who is a Bencher ex-officio shall be null and void ? and the election shall be declared as if such votes had not been cast. R. S. O. 1877, c. 138, s. 18.

21. In the event of an elector placing more than thirty names on his voting paper, the first thirty only shall be counted, notwithstanding any of the thirty persons so named may be ineligible for election from any cause whatever. R. S. O. 1877, c. 138, s. 19.

22. Upon the completion of the scrutiny the Secretary shall forthwith declare the result of the election and report the same to the Society, and shall cause the names to be published in the next two issues of the *Ontario Gazette*. R. S. O. 1877, c. 138, s. 20.

23. The Benchers of the Society may make such regulations as they consider expedient, not contrary to the provisions of this Act,

10

for regulating the procedure under the preceding sections of this Act, and for the remuneration of the scrutineers. R. S. O. 1877, c. 138, s. 21.

24. The voting papers belonging to any election shall not be destroyed until after all petitions in respect to such election have been decided, but the same shall together with all other papers in connetion with the said election be retained by the Secretary R. S. O. 1877, c. 138, s. 22.

25. No person shall sign the name of any other person to a voting paper, under this Act, or alter, or add to or falsify, or fill up any blank in a voting paper signed by another person, or deliver or cause to be delivered, or send or cause to be sent, by post or otherwise, to the Secretary, a false voting paper, or a voting paper which has been added to, or falsified or in which a blank has been filled up after the same was signed. R. S. O. 1877, c. 138, s. 23.

26. In the event of there being no Secretary for the time being of the Law Society at the time at which any election under this Act is to be held, or in the event of the Secretary being unable from illness or other unavoidable cause to act at the elections, then and in such case the Treasurer for the time being of the Law Society shall appoint under his hand some other person to act as Secretary, and the person so appointed shall perform all the duties of the Secretary, as prescribed by this Act. R. S. O. 1877, c. 138, s. 24.

27. The persons so elected Benchers as aforesaid shall take office on the first day of Easter Term following their election, and shall hold office until the beginning of the fifth Easter Term after they have entered on their said office, or till the election of their successors. R. S. O. 1877, c. 138, s. 25.

28. The seat of a Bencher, who has failed to attend the meetings of the Benchers for three consecutive Terms, shall at the expiration of the said period become vacant. R. S. O. 1877, c. 138, s. 26.

29. The majority of the Benchers present at any meeting in the first Easter Term after their election, may appoint a committee of their number to enter upon any inquiry with respect to the due election of any of the said Benchers whose election or elections may be petitioned against by any member of the Bar who voted at the election of such Bencher or Benchers, and, after such inquiry, to report such Bencher or Benchers as duly or not duly elected or qualified according to the fact, and, if necessary, to report the name or names in the next in order of votes of the duly qualified members of the Bar, in lieu of the person or persons petitioned against and reported not duly elected or qualified ; and on the confirmation of the report by the majority of Benchers (other than those petitioned against) present at any meeting for that purpose, the person or persons so reported, in lieu of those petitioned against as aforesaid shall be taken and deemed to be the duly elected and qualified Bencher or Benchers. R. S. O. 1877, c. 138, s. 27.

30. No petition against the return of a Bencher shall be entertained unless the petition is filed with the Secretary of the Law Society at least ten days before the first day of Easter Term next succeeding the election, and shall contain a statement of the grounds on which the election is disputed, and unless a copy of the petition is served upon the Bencher whose election is disputed at least ten days before the first day of the said Easter Term ; and no grounds

not mentioned in the petition shall be gone into on the hearing of the petition. R. S. O. 1877, c. 138, s. 28.

31. On such notice being duly filed as aforesaid, the Benchers shall during the first week of the Easter Term succeeding the election, appoint a day for the hearing of the petition, and give notice of such day to the petitioner and to the person whose return is disputed ; but all such petitions shall be finally disposed of during the said Easter Term. R. S. O. 1877, c. 138, s. 29.

32. Any person petitioning against the return of a Bencher shall deposit with the Secretary of the Law Society the sum of $100 to meet any cost which such Bencher may be put to in the opinion of the committee before which the petition is heard ; and the committee shall have power in the event of such petition being dismissed, to award such sum to be paid to the Bencher petitioned against as in their opinion is just ; and shall have power in their discretion in the event of such Bencher being decided to be not duly elected or qualified, to award costs to the petitioner ; and the costs so awarded shall be recoverable in any Court of competent jurisdiction. R. S. O. 1877, c. 138, s. 31.

33. The Benchers shall, on the first meeting after their election, proceed to elect one of their body as Treasurer, who shall be the President of the Society ; and such Treasurer shall hold office until the appointment of his successor ; and the election of Treasurer shall take place on the first Saturday of Easter Term in every year ; provided that the retiring Treasurer shall be eligible for re-election. R. S. O. 1877, c. 138, s. 32.

34. In case of the failure in any instance to elect the requisite number of duly qualified Benchers, according to the provisions of this Act, or in case of any vacancy caused by the death or resignation of any Bencher, or by any other cause, then it shall be the duty of the remaining Benchers, with all convenient speed, at a meeting to be specially called for the purpose, and to be held during the next Term thereafter, to supply the deficiency in the number of Benchers failed to be elected as aforesaid, or caused by any of the means aforesaid, by appointing to such vacant place or places, as the same may occur, any person or persons duly qualified under the provisions of this Act to be elected as a Bencher or Benchers ; and the person or persons so elected shall hold office for the residue of the period for which the other Benchers have been elected. R. S O 1877, c. 138, s. 33.

POWERS OF THE BENCHERS.

35. The Benchers may from time to time in Convocation make rules for the government of the Law Society, and other purposes connected therewith, under the inspection of the Visitors. R. S. O. 1877, c. 138. s. 34.

36. On the hearing of any election petition or upon any inquiry by a committee the Benchers or committee shall have power to examine witnesses under oath ; and a summons under the hand of the Treasurer of the Law Society, or under the hand of three Benchers, for the attendance of a witness, shall have all the force of a subpœna ; and any witness not attending in obedience thereto, shall be liable to attachment in the High Court. R. S. O. 1877, c. 138, s. 30.

37. The Benchers may appoint such officers and servants as may be necessary for the management of the business of the said Law Society. R. S. O. 1877, c. 138, s. 35.

38. The Benchers may make rules for the improvement of legal education ; and may appoint readers and lecturers with salaries; and may impose fees and prescribe rules for the attendance of students and articled clerks at such readings or lectures, and for examinations thereon, as condition to call to the Bar, or admission as Solicitor ; and may establish scholarships in connection therewith; and may for proficiency at examination, by rules to be established specially in that respect, diminish the number of years of studentship on the books of the Society, or under articles of clerkship, but so as not to reduce the number of years for call to the Bar or admission as Solicitor to less than three years. R. S. O. 1877, c. 138, s. 36.

39. The Benchers shall have the power heretofore exercised to call and admit to the practice of the law as a Barrister any person duly qualified to be so admitted, according to the provisions of law and the rules of the Society. R. S. O. 1877, c. 138, s. 37.

40. The Benchers may from time to time make all necessary rules, regulations and by-laws and dispense therewith from time to time to meet the special circumstances of any special case respecting the admission of students-at-law, the periods and conditions of study, the call or admission of Barristers to practice the law, and all other matters relating to the discipline and honor of the Bar. R. S. O. 1877, c. 138, s. 38.

41. The Benchers with the approbation of the Visitors shall from time to time make such rules as they consider necessary for conducting the examination of persons applying to be admitted as Solicitors, as well touching the articles and service, and the several certificates required by law to be produced by them before their admission, as to the fitness and capacity of such persons to act as Solicitors ; and the Society may from time to time nominate and appoint Examiners for conducting such examinations. R. S. O. 1877, c. 138, s. 39. *See also* Cap. 147, s. 9.

42. In any of the foregoing cases where it appears to the Benchers expedient for purposes of further inquiry or investigation, they may suspend, for a period not exceeding twelve months, their final decision in respect to the granting or refusal of the certificate. R. S. O. 1877, c. 138, s. 40.

43. The Benchers from time to time may also make all necessary rules, regulations and by-laws, and dispense therewith from time to time, to meet the special circumstances of any special case respecting the service of articled clerks, the period and conditions of such service, and the admission of Solicitors to practice in the Courts, and all other matters relating to the discipline and practice of such Solicitors and articled clerks. R. S. O. 1877, c. 138, s. 41.

44. Whenever a person, being a Barrister, or a Solicitor of the Supreme Court of Ontario, or a Student-at-Law, or Solicitor's Clerk serving under articles, has been or may hereafter, be found by the Benchers of the Law Society, after due inquiry by a committee of their number or otherwise, guilty of professional misconduct, or of conduct unbecoming a Barrister, Solicitor, Student-at-Law, or articled Clerk, it shall be lawful for the said Benchers in Convocation to disbar any such Barrister, and to resolve that any such Solicitor is unworthy to practise as such Solicitor; to expel from the society, and the membership thereof, such Student or articled Clerk, and to strike his name from the books of the Society; and to refuse either absolutely or for a limited period to admit such articled Clerk to the usual examinations, or to grant him the certificate of fitness necessary to enable him to be admitted to practice. 44 V. c. 17, s. 1.

45. Upon a Barrister being disbarred as aforesaid, all his rights and privileges as a Barrister-at-Law shall thenceforth cease and determine, and notice of his being disbarred shall forthwith be given by the Secretary of the Law Society to the High Court. 44 V. c. 17, s. 2.

46. Upon its being resolved by Convocation that a Solicitor is unworthy to practise, a copy of the resolution shall forthwith be communicated to the High Court, and thereupon, without any formal motion, an order of the said Court may be drawn up, striking such Solicitor off the rolls: Provided that such Solicitor may at any time afterwards apply to the said Court to be restored to practice, as heretofore. 44 V. c. 17, s. 3.

47. Any Powers which the Visitors of the Law Society may have in the said matters of discipline, are hereby vested in the Benchers of the Law Society, and the powers by the preceding three sections of this Act given to the said Benchers may be exercised by them without reference to, or concurrence in, by the Visitors. 44 V. c. 17, s. 4.

LAW BENEVOLENT FUND.

48. The Benchers may by by-law establish a fund for the benefit of the widows and orphans of Barristers and Solicitors, and of persons who have been such, to be called "The Law Benevolent Fund," and may make all necessary rules and regulations for the management and investment of the said fund, and the terms of subscription and appropriation thereof, and the conditions under which the widows and orphans of such persons shall be entitled to share in the said fund. R. S. O. 1877, c. 138, s. 43.

REPORTERS.

49.—(1) The Benchers may from time to time appoint such persons, being members of the Law Society, of the degree of Barrister-at-Law, as they may think proper, to be editors and reporters of the decisions of the Court of Appeal and the High Court.

(2) Such persons shall hold office at the pleasure of the said Benchers, and shall be amenable to them in Convocation for the correct and faithful discharge of their respective duties, according to such regulations as the said Benchers may from time to time make in respect thereof. R. S. O. 1877, c. 138, s. 44.

50. The Benchers shall make regulations for printing and publishing the reports of the said decisions, and the distribution of the reports, and the price and mode of issuing thereof, and all such other regulations in respect thereto, as they may at any time consider necessary; and any profits arising from the reports shall form part of the general funds of the Law Society. R. S. O. 1877, c. 138, s. 45.

51. The Benchers shall from time to time determine the salaries to be allowed to the editors and reporters, and shall pay the same out of the general funds of the Society. R. S. O. 1877, c. 138, s. 46.

52. The fees payable by Barristers, as term fees, and on call to the Bar, and by Solicitors on admission as Solicitors, and for the annual certificate to practice, and by Students and articled Clerks on admission as such, and on examinations and attendance on lectures and readings, shall be paid into the general funds of the Law Society, and shall be such as the Law Society by rule from time to time prescribes. R. S. O. 1877, c. 138, s. 47. *See also* Cap. 147, s. 16 (4).

53. The Benchers shall, during Hilary Term in every year, furnish to every member of the Law Society entitled to vote at the election of Benchers, a statement in detail of the revenue and expenditure of the Law Society, for the year ending the thirty-first day of December preceding each statement, and the same to be first duly audited by auditors appointed by said Benchers to audit and report upon the finances of the Law Society. R. S. O. 1877, c. 138, s. 48.

SCHEDULE.

(Section 9.)

FORM OF VOTING PAPER.

Law Society Election, 18 .

I, , of the in the County of
, Barrister-at-Law, do hereby declare—

1. That the signiture affixed hereto is my proper handwriting.

2. That I vote for the following persons as Benchers of the Law Society:

A. B., of the	, in the County of
C. D., of the	, in the County of
E. F., of the	, in the County of
G. H., of the	, in the County of
I. J. of the	, in the County of
etc.	etc.

3. That I have signed no other voting paper at this election.

4. That this voting paper was executed on the day of the date thereof.

Witness my hand, this day of , A. D. 18 .

R. S. O. 1877, c. 138, Sched.

An Act respecting Barristers-at-Law.

[Rev. Stat. Ont. 1887, Chap. 146.]

HER MAJESTY, by and with the advice and consent of the Legislative Assembly of the Province of Ontario enacts as follows :—

1. Subject to any rules, regulations or by-laws made by the Benchers of the Law Society of Upper Canada under *The Act respecting the Law Society of Upper Canada*, the following persons, and no others, may be admitted to practise at the Bar in Her Majesty's Courts in Ontario :

1. Any person of the age of twenty-one years, who, having been entered of and admitted into the "Law Society of Upper Canada" as a student of the laws, has been standing on the books thereof for five years, and has conformed himself to the rules of the Society ;

2. Any person who has been admitted into and stands on the books of the Law Society of Upper Canada, as a student of the laws of three years, and has conformed himself to the rules of said Society, and has, prior to the date of his admission to the said Society, and to the books of the said Society as a student, actually taken and had conferred upon him the degree of Bachelor of Arts or Bachelor of Law in any of the Universities of the United Kingdom of Great Britain and Ireland, or of any University or College in this Province or in the Province of Quebec, having power to grant degrees; R. S. O. 1877, c. 139, s. 1, (1, 2).

3. Any person who has been duly called to the Bar of England, Scotland or Ireland (excluding the Bar of Courts of merely local jurisdiction)—when the Inn of Court or other authority having power to call or admit to the Bar by which such person was called or admitted, extends the same privilege to Barristers from Ontario—on producing sufficient evidence of such call or admission and testimonials of good character and conduct to the satisfaction of the Law Society. 48 V. c. 30, s. 1.

4. Any person who has been duly authorized to practise as an Advocate, Barrister, Attorney, Solicitor and Proctor at Law, in all Courts of Justice in Quebec, or who has been found capable and qualified, and entitled to receive a diploma for that purpose under the provisions of the Acts respecting the incorporation of the Bar of Quebec, or who has been duly registered as a clerk and studied during the periods for study respectively required under the provisions of the said Acts, on producing sufficient evidence thereof, and also on producing testimonials of good character, and undergoing an examination in the law of Ontario, to the satisfaction of the Law Society of Upper Canada, and upon his entering himself of the said Society, and conforming to all the rules and regulations thereof ;

5. Any person who has been duly called to the Bar of any of Her Majesty's Superior Courts in any of Her Majesty's Provinces of North America in which the same privilege would be extended to Barristers from Ontario, and who produces sufficient evidence of such call and testimonials of good character and conduct to the satisfaction of the Law Society. R. S. O. 1877, c. 139, s. 1 (4, 5).

QUEEN'S COUNSEL.

2. It was and is lawful for the Lieutenant-Governor by letters patent, under the Great Seal of the Province of Ontario, to appoint from among the members of the Bar of Ontario, such persons as he may deem right to be, during pleasure, Provincial officers under the names of Her Majesty's Counsel learned in the Law for the Province of Ontario. R. S. O. 1877, c. 139, s. 2.

3. The following members of the Bar of this Province shall have precedence in the Courts of this Province in the following order:

1. The Attorney-General of Canada for the time being;

2. The Attorney-General of Ontario for the time being;

3. The members of the said Bar who have filled the offices of Attorney-General for the late Province of Upper Canada, or Attorney-General of the Dominion of Canada, or Attorney-General of this Province, according to seniority of appointment as such Attorney-General;

4. The members of the said Bar who have filled the office of Solicitor-General for Upper Canada according to seniority of appointment as such Solicitor-General; and

5. The members of the Bar who were, before the first day of July, in the year of our Lord, 1867, appointed Her Majesty's Counsel for Upper Canada, so long as they are such Counsel, according to seniority of appointment as such Counsel. R. S. O. 1877, c. 139, s. 3.

4. The Lieutenant-Governor by letters patent under the Great Seal of Ontario may grant to any member of the Bar a patent of precedence in the said Courts. R. S. O. 1877, c. 139, s. 4.

5. Members of the Bar from time to time appointed after the 1st day of July, in the year of Our Lord, 1867, to be Her Majesty's Counsel for the Province, and members of the Bar to whom, from time to time, patents of precedence are granted shall severally have such precedence in the said Courts as may be assigned to them by letters patent, which may be issued by the Lieutenant-Governor under the Great Seal. R. S. O. 1877, c. 139, s. 5.

6. The remaining members of the Bar shall, as between themselves, have precedence in the said Courts in the order of their call to the Bar. R. S. O. 1877, c. 139, s. 6.

7. Nothing in this Act contained shall in any wise affect or alter any rights of precedence which may appertain to any member of the Bar when acting as Counsel for Her Majesty, or for any Attorney-General of Her Majesty, in any matter depending in the name of Her Majesty or of the Attorney-General before the said Courts, but such right and precedence shall remain as if this Act had not been passed. R. S. O. 1877, c. 139, s. 7.

An Act respecting Solicitors.

[Rev. Stat. Ont. 1887, Chap. 147.]

HER MAJESTY, by and with the advice and consent of the Legislative Assembly of the Province of Ontario, enacts as follows :—

SOLICITORS TO BE ADMITTED AND ENROLLED.

1. Unless admitted and enrolled and duly qualified to act as a Solicitor, no person shall act as a Solicitor in any Court of Civil or Criminal Jurisdiction or before any Justice of the Peace, or shall as such sue out any writ or process, or commence, carry on, solicit or defend any action, or proceeding in the name of any other person, or in his own name. R. S. O. 1877, c. 140, s. 1.

[See as to Division Courts, Rev. Stat., c. 51, s. 120.]

WHO MAY BE ADMITTED.

2.—(1) All persons heretofore admitted as Solicitors or Attorneys of, or by law empowered to practise in, any Court the jurisdiction of which is now vested in the High Court shall be called Solicitors of the Supreme Court of Ontario, and shall be entitled to the same privileges, and be subject to the same obligations, so far as circumstances will permit, as they were entitled or subject to prior to the 22ud day of August, 1881.

(2) All persons who from time to time, if *The Ontario Judicature Act, 1881,* had not passed, would have been entitled to be admitted as Solicitors or Attorneys of, or been by law empowered to practise in, any such Courts, shall be entitled to be admitted on payment of the fees mentioned in section 12 and shall be so admitted by any

Divisional Court, and shall be Solicitors of the Supreme Court of Ontario.

(3) Any Solicitors or Attorneys to whom this section applies shall be deemed to be officers of the Supreme Court; and that Court, and the High Court of Justice and the Court of Appeal respectively, or any Division or Judge thereof, may exercise the same jurisdiction in respect of such Solicitors or Attorneys as any one of the Superior Courts or a Judge thereof might, previously to the 22nd day of August, 1881, have exercised in respect of any Solicitor or Attorney admitted to practice therein. 44 V. c. 5, s. 74.

3. Subject to the provisions hereinafter contained and to any rules and regulations made by the Benchers of the Law Society of Upper Canada, under *The Act respecting the Law Society of Upper Canada,* the following persons and no others may be admitted and enrolled as Solicitors:

1. Any person who has been bound by contract in writing to a practicising Solicitor in Ontario to serve and has served him as his clerk for five years ;

2. Any person who has actually taken and had conferred upon him the degree of Bachelor or Master of Arts, or of Bachelor or Doctor of Laws, in any of the Universities of the United Kingdom of Great Britain and Ireland, or of this Province or the Province of Quebec having power to grant degrees, and has, after having taken and had conferred upon him such degree, been bound by contract in writing to a practising Solicitor in Ontario to serve and has served him as his clerk for three years ;

3. Any person who has been duly called to practise at the Bar of Ontario, or who has been duly called to practise at the Bar of any of Her Majesty's Superior Courts not having merely local jurisdiction in England, Scotland or Ireland, and has been bound by con·tract in writing to a practising Solicitor in Ontario to serve and has served him as his clerk for three years ;

4. Any person duly and lawfully sworn, admitted and enrolled a Solicitor of Her Majesty's Supreme Court of Judicature in Eng·land or Ireland, or who has been Writer to the Signet or Solicitor in the Supreme Courts in Scotland, and has been bound by contract in writing to a practising Solicitor in Ontario to serve and has served him as his clerk for one year ;

5. Any Attorney or Solicitor of any of Her Majesty's Superior Courts of Law or Equity in any of Her Majesty's Colonies wherein the Common Law of England is the Common Law of the land, and who has been bound by contract in writing to a practising Solicitor in Ontario, to serve and has served him as his clerk for one year. R. S. O. 1877, c. 140, s. 2.

4. The High Court may in its discretion admit as Solicitors any persons who have been called to the degree of Barrister-at-Law under the provisions of sub-section 4 of section 1 of *The Act respecting Barristers-at-Law,* on their producing such evidence and testimon·ials, and undergoing an examination in the law of Ontario under the direction of the Law Society of Upper Canada to the satisfaction of the Court. R. S. O. 1877, c. 140, s. 3.

SERVICE OF ARTICLED CLERKS.

5. Subject to the powers of the Benchers of the Law Society of Upper Canada to make rules, regulations and by-laws, under *The Act respecting the Law Society of Upper Canada,* the following enactments are made with respect to the service of articled clerks :—

1. Whenever any person has been by bound contract, in writing, to serve as a clerk to a Solicitor, such contract with the affidavit of execution thereof annexed thereto, shall within three months next after the execution of the contract be filed with the Registrar of the Common Pleas Division of the High Court, who shall endorse and sign upon the contract and affidavit a memorandum of the day of filing thereof, and every assignment of such contract, together with an affidavit of the execution thereof annexed thereto, shall be filed in like manner within the like period of three months next after the execution thereof. Every such affidavit shall state the date of the execution of the articles or assignment, as the case may be, by the parties thereto respectively.

2. In case the contract or assignment (as the case may be) with the affidavit of execution annexed thereto, is not filed within three months after the date of the contract or assignment, the same may nevertheless be filed with either of the officers before mentioned, but the service of the clerk shall be reckoned only from the date of the filing, unless the Law Society in its discretion for special reasons in any particular case otherwise orders.

3. Every person authorized to practice as a Solicitor may have under contract in writing four clerks at one time, and no more ; and no Solicitor shall have any clerk bound as aforesaid, after the Solicitor has discontinued practising as, or carrying on the business of, a Solicitor, nor whilst the Solicitor is employed as a writer or clerk by any other Solicitor ; and the service by an articled clerk to a Solicitor under any such circumstances, shall not be deemed good service under the articles.

4. In case any Solicitor before the determination of the contract of a clerk bound to him as aforesaid, has become bankrupt, or taken the benefit of any Act for the relief of insolvent debtors, or having been imprisoned for debt has remained in prison for the space of twenty-one days, the High Court may, upon the application of the clerk, order the contract to be discharged or assigned to such person, upon such terms, and in such manner as the Court thinks fit.

5. If a Solicitor, to whom a clerk has been so bound, dies before the expiration of the term for which the clerk became bound, or if he discontinues practice as a Solicitor, or if the contract is by the consent of the parties cancelled, or in case the clerk is legally discharged before the expiration of the term by any rule or order of the Court, the clerk may be bound by another contract in writing, to serve as clerk to any other practicing Solicitor during the residue of his said term ; and in case an affidavit is duly made and filed of the execution of such last mentioned contract within the time and in the manner hereinbefore directed, and subject to the like regulations with respect to the original contract and the affidavit of its execution, due service under such second or subsequent contract shall be deemed sufficient. R. S. O. 1877, c. 140, s. 4.

CONDITIONS OF ADMISSION AS SOLICITOR.

6.—(1) Subject to the rules, regulations, and by-laws made by the Benchers of the Law Society of Upper Canada, under *The Act respecting the Law Society of Upper Canada*, no person above mentioned shall be admitted and enrolled as a Solicitor unless :

(a) He has during the time specified in his contract of service duly served thereunder, and has during the whole of such term of service been actually employed in the proper practice or business of a Solicitor by the Solicitor to whom he has been bound at the place where such Solicitor has continued to reside, during such term or (with his consent) by the professional agent of the Solicitor in Toronto, for a part of the said term, not exceeding one year ; nor unless

(b) He has after the expiration of such term of service been examined and sworn in the manner hereinafter directed ; nor unless

(c) He has, at least fourteen days next before the first day of the Term in which he seeks admission, left with the Secretary of the Law Society his contract of service, and any assignment thereof and affidavits of the execution of the same respectively, and his own affidavit of due service thereunder, and a certificate of the Solicitor to whom he was bound, or his agent as aforesaid, of such due service, and (in the case of a person who has been called to the Bar or taken a degree as hereinbefore mentioned), a certificate of his having been so called to the Bar or taken such degree or a duly authenticated certified copy of such certificate.

(2.) The affidavits shall be in the form approved of by the Visitors of the Law Society, and shall by the applicant be delivered to the Law Society upon his application to be examined.

(3.) In case the contract of service, assignment (if any) affidavits and certificate of due service, or any of them, cannot be produced, then, on application to be made to the Law Society, by a petition verified by affidavit, to be left with the Secretary of the Society, at least fourteen days next before the first day of the Term on which the applicant seeks admission, the Society on being satisfied of such fact may, in its discretion, dispense with the production of such contract, assignment, affidavits and certificate of due service, or any of them, and may, notwithstanding such non-production, grant the certificates provided for in section 10 of this Act.

(4.) The Benchers of the Law Society may allow any clerk under articles to a practising Solicitor, as part of his term of service, all and every period of time that such clerk may have been employed in the Militia Service when the Militia are called out for actual service.

(5) No candidate shall be admitted unless he makes and subscribes the oath or affirmation following :

"I, A. B., do swear (or solemnly affirm as the case may be) that I will truly and honestly demean myself in the practice of a Solicitor according to the best of my knowledge and ability; So help me God." R. S. O. 1887, c. 140, s. 5.

EXAMINATIONS.

7. Subject to any rules, regulations, and by-laws made by the Benchers of the Law Society of Upper Canada, under *The Act respecting the Law Society of Upper Canada*, the following enactments are made with respect to the examination of articled clerks and candidates for admission as Solicitors :

1. The Benchers of the Law Society of Upper Canada may by regulation require that articled clerks shall pass a preliminary examination ; and the term of service under articles to entitle each articled clerk to be admitted as a Solicitor shall date only from the passing of such examination.

2. Notwithstanding anything in this Act contained, no persons being of either of the classes of persons mentioned in sub-sections 1

and 2 of section 2 of this Act shall be admitted or enrolled as a Solicitor, unless he has at some time during the year next but two before the time of his final examination, and at some time not less than one year thereafter and during the year next but one before the time of his final examination, passed examinations to the satisfaction of the said Benchers.

3. In case any person is prevented by illness or other unavoidable cause, from presenting himself for, or fails to pass either of the examinations by this section required, within the time specified, the Benchers may, in their discretion, permit such person to pass such examination at other times; but not less than nine months shall elapse between the first and the second of such examinations not less than nine months shall elapse between the second of such examinations and the final examination. R. S. O. 1877, c. 140, s.6.

8. Subject to the rules and regulations of the Law Society of Upper Canada, as aforesaid, no candidate for admission being of the class of persons respectively mentioned in sub-sections 3, 4 and 5 of section 2 of this Act, shall be admitted unless,

1. He publishes in the *Ontario Gazette*, at least two months previously, notice of his intention to apply for admission.

2. Nor (except in the case of a person called to the Bar of Ontario), unless such candidate, at least fourteen days before the first day of such Term, leaves with the Secretary of the Law Society:

   (a) In the case of a Barrister not being a Barrister of Ontario—a certificate under the seal of the Society, or Inn of Court in England, Scotland or Ireland, of which he is a member, duly attested under the proper hand of the proper officer thereof, that he has been duly called to the Bar, and was at the date of such certificate on the books of such Society or Inn of Court; and also an affidavit of the applicant to the satisfaction of the Benchers of the Law Society, that since his admission to the Bar, no application to any Society or Inn of Court has been made against such person to disbar him or otherwise to disqualify him from further practice for misconduct in such his capacity of Barrister;

   (b) And in the case of an Attorney or Solicitor—a certificate under the seal of the proper Court or Courts, duly attested under the hand of the proper officer thereof, that he was duly admitted and enrolled as such Attorney or Solicitor, and was at the date of such certificate on the Roll of Attorneys or Solicitors of such Court or Courts; and also, an affidavit of the applicant, that since his admission as aforesaid no application to any such Court or Courts (as the case may be) has been made against such person to strike him off the Roll of any such Court, or otherwise to disqualify him in the capacity of Attorney or Solicitor;

(3.) The certificates respectively shall bear date within three months of the first day of the term during which the application is made. R. S. O. 1877, c. 140, s. 7.

9. The Benchers of the Law Society of Upper Canada with the approbation of the Visitors shall from time to time make such rules as they consider necessary for conducting the examination of persons applying to be admitted as Solicitors, as well touching the articles and service, and the several certificates required by law to be produced by them before their admission, as touching the fitness and capacity of such persons to act as Solicitors; and the Society may from time to time nominate and appoint examiners for conducting such examinations. R. S. O. 1877, c. 140, s. 8. *See also* Cap. 145, s. 41.

10. The Benchers of the Law Society, upon proof to their satisfaction of the requisites of this Act having been complied with, shall examine and enquire by such ways and means as they think proper, touching the fitness and capacity of any applicant for admission to act as a Solicitor; and if satisfied by such examination, or by the certificate of the examiners mentioned in section 9 of this Act, that such person is duly qualified, fit, and competent to act as a Solicitor, the Society shall give a certificate under the corporate seal of the said Society of the due service under contract in writing, of such person, and of his fitness and capacity, and of his having duly complied with the requirements of this Act, and that he is in all respects duly qualified to be admitted as a Solicitor. R. S. O. 1877, c. 140, s. 9.

11. Upon production to one of the Judges of the High Court annexed to such certificate of the original contract of service and any assignments thereof, and the affidavits of due service thereunder, and all other certificates hereinbefore required, such Judge shall endorse his fiat of admission upon the certificate of the Law Society; and thereupon the High Court may, in addition to the oath of allegiance, administer to such person in open Court the oath hereinbefore directed to be taken by Solicitors, and after such oaths taken may cause him to be admitted and his name to be enrolled as a Solicitor, which admission shall be signed by the Registrar of one of the Divisions of the High Court, and the documents upon which the admission has been obtained shall be filed and retained of record in the office of the Court. R. S. O. 1877, c. 140, s. 10.

FEI S.

12. The following fees, and no other, shall be payable to the Registrar for the Crown in stamps under this Act, subject to the provisions of *The Act respecting Law Stamps*, that is to say :

1. On filing Articles and Assignments (if any) and every affidavit of execution of such Articles, and making the endorsement required by this Act.................... $0 50
2. For fiat, admission, oath and certificate................ 5 50
R. S. O. 1877, c. 140, s. 12. *See the Tariff.*

ANNUAL CERTIFICATES.

13. The Registrar of one of the Divisions of the High Court, shall annually, during the Vacation after Trinity Term, deliver to the Secretary or at his office in Osgoode Hall, certified under his hand and the seal of the said High Court a copy of so much of the Roll as contains the names of Solicitors admitted to practice subsequently to the last return made to the said Secretary. R. S. O. 1877, c. 140, s. 13.

14. The Secretary shall enter all such certified copies in a book to be kept in his office for that purpose, affixing to each name a number following in consecutive order the numbers affixed to the names previously entered. R. S. O. 1877, c. 140, s. 14.

15. The Secretary shall, in another book to be kept in his office for that purpose, enter all the names contained in the copies so transmitted to him, alphabetically arranged, with a reference to the number of each name on the Roll ; and shall, annually on or before the first day of February, put up in his office and also in the office of each of the Registrars of the High Court an alphabetical list certified by him, under his hand, of all Solicitors who have taken out their certificates for the current year, and shall from time to time add to the list put up in his own office the name of each Solicitor who takes out a certificate at a subsequent period of the year, noting thereon the time when the certificate was taken out. R. S. O. 1877, c. 140, s. 15.

16.—(1) Every practicing Solicitor shall obtain from the Secretary of the Law Society, annually, before the last day of Michaelmas Term, a certificate under the seal of the said Society stating that he is a practicing Solicitor in the High Court.

(2) Such certificates shall be issued by the Secretary of the Law Society, under the seal of the Society, according to the list of names appearing in the copy of the Roll of Solicitors certified to the said Secretary under section 13 of this Act.

(3) Upon the payment of all fees and dues payable by such Solicitor to the said Society, the Secretary shall write his name on the margin of the certificate, with the date thereof, and the certificate shall be taken as issued only from such date.

(4) The Law Society shall determine what fees shall be payable for certificates. R. S. O 1877, c. 140, s. 16.

17. No certificate shall be issued to any Solicitor, who is indebted to the Society, for any Term or other fee payable to the Society, nor until the annual fee for each certificate prescribed by the rules of the Society is paid. R. S. O. 1877, c. 140, s. 17.

18. No Solicitor, admitted as aforesaid, need take out any such certificate until the Michaelmas Term next following his admission. R. S. O. 1877, c. 140, s. 18.

19.—(1) If a Solicitor omits to take out such annual certificate in Michaelmas Term, he shall not be entitled thereto until he pays to the Law Society not only the certificate fee, so appointed as aforesaid, together with any other fees or dues which he owes to the Society, but also an additional sum by way of penalty, as follows :

(2) If such certificate is not taken out before the first day of Hilary Term, the further sum of $6 ; if not before the first day of Easter Term, the further sum of $9; and, if not before the first day of Trinity Term, the further sum of $12. R. S. O. 1877, c. 140, s. 19.

20. If a Solicitor, or any member of a firm of Solicitors, either in his own name or in the name of any member of his firm, practices in the High Court, without such certificate being taken out by him, and by each member of his firm, he shall forfeit the sum of $40, which forfeiture shall be paid to the Law Society for the uses thereof, and may be recovered in the High Court. R. S. O. 1877, c. 140, s. 20.

21. If a Solicitor practices in the High Court or in a County Court without such certificate in each and any year of his practice he shall be liable to be suspended by order of the High Court from practice for such offence, for a period of not less than three nor more than six months, and to continue so suspended until the fee

upon his certificate for the year in which he so practiced without certificate, is, together with a penalty of $40, paid to the Law Society. R. S. O. 1877, c. 140, s. 21.

22.—(1) Each of the Registrars of the High Court and each Deputy Clerk of the Crown and Pleas, and each Deputy Registrar, when the said offices are not held by the same person, shall, at the commencement of each year, make out a list of the names of every Solicitor who by the papers or proceedings filed or had in their respective offices appears to have practiced as such Solicitor at any time during the preceding year ending with the thirty-first day of December.

(2) Each of the said officers shall, on or before the first day of Hilary Term in the year next to that for which they are made up, deliver or hand such lists to the Secretary at Osgoode Hall, certified under their respective hands and seals. R. S. O. 1877, c. 140, ss. 22, 23.

23. In case a Solicitor is a prisoner in any gaol or prison he shall not during his confinement therein, or within the limits thereof, commence, prosecute or defend as such Solicitor any action in any Court, nor act in any matter in bankruptcy or insolvency; and any Solicitor so practicing, and any solicitor permitting or empowering him so to practice in his name, shall be guilty of a contempt of the Court in which any such proceedings take place, and (upon the application of any person complaining thereof) shall be punishable by such Court accordingly; and such Solicitor shall be incapable of maintaining any action for the recovery of any fee, reward or disbursement for or in respect of any matter or thing done by him, whilst a prisoner as aforesaid, in his own name or in the name of any other Solicitor. R. S. O. 1877, c. 140, s. 24.

24. In case a Solicitor wilfully and knowingly acts as the professional agent of any person not duly qualified to act as a Solicitor, or suffers his name to be used in any such agency on account of or for the profit of an unqualified person, or sends any process to such person, or does any other act to enable such person to practice in any respect as a Solicitor, knowing him not to be duly qualified, and in case complaint is made thereof in a summary way to the High Court, and proof is made upon oath to the satisfaction of the Court, the Solicitor so offending may, in the discretion of the Court, be struck off the Roll and disabled from practicing as such Solicitor; and the Court may also commit such unqualified person so having practiced as aforesaid to any common gaol or prison for any term not exceeding one year. R. S. O. 1877, c. 140, s. 25.

25. The High Court may strike the name of any Solicitor off the Roll of Solicitors of the Court, for default by him in payment of moneys recived by him as a Solicitor. R. S. O. 1877, c. 140, s. 26.

26.—In case any person, unless himself a plaintiff or defendant in the proceeding, commences, prosecutes or defends in his own name, or that of any other person, any action or proceeding without being dmitted and enrolled as aforesaid, he shall be incapable of recovering any fee, reward or disbursements on account thereof; and such ioffence shall be a contempt of the Court in which such proceeding has been commenced, carried on or defended, and punishable accordingly. R. S. O. 1877, c. 140, s. 27.

27. No Solicitor shall practice in any Court in Ontario, either in his own name or by his partner, deputy or agent, or in the name of any other person, or otherwise, directly or indirectly, while he holds, possesses, practices, carries on or conducts any of the offices of Registrar of the Court of Appeal, Registrar of any Division of the High Court, Deputy Clerk of the Crown and Pleas, Clerk of a County Court, or Clerk of a Division Court, and every such person so practicing, shall be subject to the forfeiture of such office, and shall, in addition thereto, be subject to a penalty of $2,000 to be recovered in an action in the High Court, to the use of Her Majesty; but nothing herein contained shall extend to any Local Master or Deputy Registrar of the High Court, who is not a Deputy Clerk of the Crown and Pleas. R. S. O. 1877, c. 140, s. 28.

28. No Solicitor shall practice in any of the Courts of Ontario during the time he is engaged in the business of a merchant, or connected by partnership, public or private, in purchasing or vending merchandise in the way of trade as a merchant, nor until twelve months after he has ceased to be such merchant or to be so engaged, or to be connected as aforesaid. R. S. O. 1877, c. 140, s. 29.

TIME LIMITED FOR STRIKING A SOLICITOR OFF THE ROLL.

29. Except in case of fraud, no person admitted and enrolled shall be struck off the Roll on account of any defect in the articles of clerkship, or in the registry thereof, or in his service thereunder, or in his admission and enrolment, unless application for striking him off the Roll is made within twelve months next after his admission and enrolment. R. S. O. 1877, c. 140, s. 30.

PROCEEDINGS IF STRUCK OFF THE ROLL.

30. Where a Solicitor is struck off the Roll of the High Court, the Registrar of the Division of the High Court in which the order is made shall certify the same under his hand and the seal of the Court to the Secretary of the Law Society, stating whether such Solicitor was struck off at his own request or otherwise, and the Secretary shall attach the certificate to the certified copy of the Roll on which the name of such person stands, and shall, in the book to be kept by him as aforesaid, make a note opposite the name of such person of his having been struck off such Roll. R. S. O. 1877, c. 140, s. 31.

SOLICITOR'S COSTS.

31. No action shall be brought for the recovery of fees, charges or disbursements, for business done by a Solicitor as such, until one month after a bill thereof, subscribed with the proper hand of such Solicitor, his executor, administrator or assignee (or, in the case of a partnership, by one of the partners, either with his own name, or with the name or style of such partnership), has been delivered to the party to be charged therewith, or sent by the post to, or left for him at his counting-house, office of business, dwelling-house, or last known place of abode, or has been enclosed in or accompanied by a letter subscribed in like manner, referring to such bill. R. S. O. 1877, c. 140, s. 32.

32. Upon the application of the party chargeable by such bill within the month the High Court or a Judge thereof, or a Judge of a County Court shall, without money being brought into Court, refer the bill and the demand thereon to be taxed by the proper officer of any of the Courts in the County in which any of the business charged

for in the bill was done, and the Court or Judge making such reference shall restrain the bringing any action for such demand pending the reference. R. S. O. 1877, c. 140, s. 33.

33. In case no application is made within the month, then the Court or Judge upon the application of either party may order a reference with such directions and conditions as he may deem proper; and may upon such terms as may be thought just restrain any action for such demand pending the reference. R. S. O. 1877, c. 140, s. 34.

34. No such reference shall be directed upon application made by the party chargeable with such bill after a verdict has been obtained or a writ of inquiry executed, or after twelve months from the time such bill was delivered, sent or left as aforesaid, except under special circumstances, to be proved to the satisfaction of the Court or Judge to whom the application for the reference is made. R. S. O. 1877, c. 140, s. 35.

35. In case either party to such reference, having due notice, refuses or neglects to attend the taxation, the officer to whom the reference is made may tax the bill *ex parte*; and in case the reference is made upon the application of either party and the party chargeable with the bill attends the taxation, the costs of the reference shall be paid according to the event of the taxation, except that if a sixth part is taxed off, the costs shall be paid by the party by whom or on whose behalf such bill was delivered; and if less than a sixth part is taxed off, then by the party chargeable with such bill, if he applied for or attended the taxation. R. S. O. 1877, c. 140, s. 36.

36. Every order for such reference shall direct the officer to whom the reference is made, to tax the costs of the reference, and to certify what, upon the reference, he finds to be due to or from either party in respect of such bill and of the costs of the reference, if payable. R. S. O. 1877, c. 140, s. 37.

37. Such officer may certify specially any circumstances relating to the bill or taxation, and the Court or Judge may thereupon make such order as may be deemed right respecting the payment of the costs of the taxation. R. S. O. 1877, c. 140, s. 38.

38. In case the reference is made when the same is not authorized except under special circumstances, as hereinbefore provided, the Court or Judge, in making the same, may give any special directions relative to the costs of the reference. R. S. O. 1877, c. 140, s. 39.

39. Where no bill has been delivered, sent or left as aforesaid, and where the bill if delivered, sent or left, might have been referred as aforesaid, any such Court or Judge may order the delivery of a bill, and may also order the delivery up of deeds or papers in the possession, custody or power of the Solicitor, his assignee or representatives, in the same manner as has heretofore been done in cases where any such business has been transacted in the Court in which such order was made. R. S. O. 1877, c. 140, s. 40.

40. In proving a compliance with this Act it shall not be necessary in the first instance to prove the contents of the bill delivered, sent or left, but it shall be sufficient to prove that a bill of fees, charges or disbursements subscribed in the manner aforesaid, or enclosed in or accompanied by such letter as foresaid, was delivered, sent or left in manner aforesaid; but the other party may show that the bill so

delivered, sent or left, was not such a bill as constituted a *bona fide* compliance with this Act. R. S. O. 1877, c. 140, s. 41.

41. A Judge of the High Court or a County Judge, on proof to his satisfaction that there is probable cause for believing that the party chargeable is about to quit Ontario, may authorize a Solicitor to commence an action for the recovery of his fees, charges or disbursements against the party chargeable therewith, although one month has not expired since the delivery of a bill as aforesaid. R. S. O. 1877, c. 140, s. 42.

42. Where any person not being chargeable as the principal party is liable to pay or has paid any bill either to the Solicitor, his assignee, or representative, or to the principal party entitled thereto, the person so paying, his assignee or representative, may make the like application for a reference thereof to taxation as the party chargeable therewith might himself have made, and in like manner, and the same proceedings shall be had thereupon, as if the application had been made by the party so chargeable. R. S. O. 1877, c. 140, s. 43.

43. In case such application is made when, under the provisions hereinbefore contained, a reference is not authorized to be made except under special circumstances, the Court or Judge to whom the application is made, may take into consideration any additional special circumstances applicable to the person making it, although such circumstances might not be applicable to the party chargeable with the bill, if he was the party making the application. R. S. O. 1877, c. 140, s. 44.

44. For the purpose of such reference upon the application of the person not being the party chargeable, or of a party interested as aforesaid, the Court or Judge may order the Solicitor, his assignee or representative, to deliver to the party making the application a copy of the bill upon payment of the costs of the copy. R. S. O. 1877, c. 140, s. 45.

45. No bill previously taxed shall be again referred, unless under the special circumstances of the case the Court or Judge to whom the application is made thinks fit to direct a re-taxation thereof. R. S. O. 1877, c. 140, s. 46.

46. The payment of any such bill as aforesaid shall in no case preclude the Court or Judge to whom application is made from referring such bill for taxation, if the application is made within twelve months after payment, and if the special circumstances of the case in the opinion of the Court or Judge appear to require the same, upon such terms and subject to such directions as to the Court or Judge seem right. R. S. O. 1877, c. 140, s. 47.

47. In all cases in which a bill is referred to be taxed, the officer to whom the reference is made, may request the proper officer of any other Court, to assist him in taxing any part of such bill, and the officer, so requested, shall thereupon tax the same, and shall have the same powers, and may receive the same fees in respect thereof, as upon a reference to him by the Court of which he is an officer, and he shall return the bill, with his opinion thereon, to the officer who so requests him to tax the same. R. S. O. 1877, c. 140, s. 48.

48.—All applications made to refer any bill to be taxed, or for the delivery of a bill, or for the delivering up of deeds, documents and papers, shall be made *In the matter of (such Solicitor)*; and upon the taxation of any such bill, the certificate of the officer by whom the bill is taxed shall, unless set aside or altered by order of a Judge, or by decree or order of Court, be final and conclusive as to the amount thereof, and payment of the amount certified to be due and directed to be paid may be enforced according to the practice of the Court in which the reference has been made. R. S. O. 1877, c. 140, s. 49.

JUDGES MAY MAKE RULES.

49. The Judges of the Supreme Court may, from time to time in accordance with the provisions of *The Judicature Act*, make such General Rules or Regulations, other than the Rules or Regulations hereinbefore referred to, as to them seem necessary and meet for carrying out the provisions of this Act. R. S. O. 1877, c. 140, s. 50.

50.—(1) Any such general rule may, as regards the mode of remuneration, prescribe that it shall be according to a scale of rates of commission or per centage, varying or not in different classes of business ; or by a gross sum ; or by a fixed sum for each document prepared or perused, without regard to length ; or in any other mode, or partly in one mode and partly in another, or others ; and may, as regards the amount of the remuneration, regulate the same with reference to all or any of the following among other considerations ; namely :—the position of the party for whom the Solicitor is concerned in any business, that is, whether as vendor or as purchaser, lessor or lessee, mortgagor or mortgagee, and the like ; the place, district, and circumstances at or in which the business or part thereof is transacted ; the amount of the capital money or of the rent to which the business relates ; the skill, labour and responsibility involved therein on the part of the Solicitor ; the number and importance of the documents prepared or perused, without regard to length ; and the average or ordinary remuneration obtained by Solicitors in like business at the passing of this Act.

(2) As long as such general rule is in operation, the taxation of bills of costs of Solicitors shall be regulated thereby. 49 V. c. 20. s. 22.

51.—(1) With respect to any business to which the preceding section relates, whether any general rule under this Act is in operation or not, it shall be competent (subject to the provisions hereinafter mentioned) for a Solicitor to make an agreement with his client, and for a client to make an agreement with his Solicitor, before or after or in the course of the transaction of such business, for the remuneration of the Solicitor, to such amount and in such manner as the Solicitor and the client think fit, either by a gross sum, or by commission or percentage, or by salary, or otherwise ; and it shall be competent for the Solicitor to accept from the client, and for the client to give to the Solicitor, remuneration accordingly.

(2) The agreement shall be in writing, signed by the person to be bound thereby or by his agent in that behalf.

(3) The agreement may, if the Solicitor and the client think fit, be made on the terms that the amount of the remuneration therein stipulated for either shall include or shall not include all or any disbursements made by the Solicitor in respect of searches, plans, travelling fees, or other matters.

(4) The agreement may be sued and recovered on, or impeached and set aside, in the like manner and on the like grounds as an

agreement not relating to the remuneration of a Solicitor, and if under any order for taxation of costs, such agreement being relied upon by the Solicitor shall be objected to by the client as unfair and unreasonable, the taxing master or officer of the Court may inquire into the facts, and certify the same to the Court; and if, upon such certificate, it shall appear to the Court or Judge that just cause has been shewn either for cancelling the agreement, or for reducing the amount payable under the same, the Court or Judge shall have power to order such cancellation or reduction, and to give all such directions, necessary or proper for the purpose of carrying the order into effect, or otherwise consequential thereon, as to the Court or Judge may seem fit.

(5) "Client," for the purposes of this section, includes any persons who, as a principal, or on behalf of another or as trustee or executor or in any other capacity, has power, express or implied, to retain or employ, and retains or employs, or is about to retain or employ, a Solicitor, and any person for the time being liable to pay to a Solicitor for his services any costs, remuneration, charges, expenses, or disbursements. 49 V. c. 20, s. 23.

52. In the absence of any general rule and so far as any such general rules do not apply the taxing officer in taxing any bill for preparing and executing any deed under Chapters 105, 106, and 107, of these Revised Statutes, in estimating the proper sum to be charged therefor, shall consider not the length of such deed, but the skill and labour employed and responsibility incurred in the preparation thereof. R. S. O. 1877, c. 102, s. 5.

PRESENT PRACTICE, AS TO ADMISSIONS NOT ALTERED.

53. Nothing in this Act contained shall interfere with the present practice as to the admission of Solicitors, nor with the jurisdiction over them as officers of Court. R. S. O. 1877, c. 140, s. 51.

An Act respecting Notaries Public.

[Rev. Stat. Ont. 1887, Chap. 153.]

HER MAJESTY, by and with the advice and consent of the Legislative Assembly of the Province of Ontario, enacts as follows:

1. The Lieutenant-Governor may, from time to time, appoint as he thinks fit under his hand and seal at arms, one or more Notaries Public for this Province   R. S. O. 1877, c. 141, s. 1.

2. Every such Notary shall have, use and exercise the power of drawing, passing, keeping and issuing all deeds and contracts, charter-parties and other mercantile transactions in this Province, and also of attesting all commercial instruments that may be brought before him for public protestation, and otherwise of acting as usual in the office of Notary, and may demand, receive and have all the rights, profits and emoluments rightfully appertaining and belonging to the said calling of Notary Public during pleasure.   R. S. O. 1877, c. 141, s. 2.

3. Every Notary Public having authority in Ontario, shall have the same powers as a commissioner appointed under *The Act respecting Commissioners for taking Affidavits and Recognizances.*   48 V. c. 16, s. 1.

4. Every Notary Public may in any part of Ontario take and receive all such affidavits and affirmations (in cases where by law affirmation is allowed) as any person desirous to make in or concerning any matter or thing depending or in anywise concerning any of the proceedings in the High Court, or in the Court of Appeal, and in any County or Division Court, or concerning any application made or depending before a Judge or Judges of any of said Courts, and in or concerning any application or matter made or pending before any Judge of any Court in this Province in which, by any statute now or hereafter in force in Ontario, such Judge is authorized to make any order, although such application or matter is not made or pending in any Court.   48 V. c. 16, s. 2.

5. Every Notary Public shall be deemed an officer of the High Court and of the Court of Appeal, and all affidavits and affirmations taken shall be of the same force as if taken before a Commissioner, and may be read and made use of as other affidavits and affirmations taken in Court.   48 V. c. 16, s. 4.

6. Any Notary Public misconducting himself in respect of the powers conferred upon him by the preceding three sections of this Act or by section 41 of *The Registry Act* shall be subject to the same penalty or punishment as a Commissioner in and for the High Court, and any power thereby conferred upon a Notary Public may be revoked in the same way and manner and to the same extent as if such power had been conferred upon him under any of the provisions of *The Act respecting Commissioners for taking Affidavits and Recognizances.*   48 V. c. 16, ss. 3, 5.

7.—(1) Any person other than a Barrister or Solicitor duly admitted as such in this Province, desirous of being appointed as a Notary Public, shall be subject to examination in regard to his qualification for the said office, by the County Court Judge of the county in which he resides, or by such other person as may from time to time be appointed in that behalf by the Lieutenant-Governor ; and no such person shall be appointed a Notary Public without a certificate from the said County Court Judge, or such other person, that he has examined the applicant and finds him qualified for the office, and that in his opinion a Notary Public is needed for the public convenience in the place where the applicant resides and intends to carry on business.

(2) The Lieutenant-Governor in Council, may from time to time make regulations for such examination and certificate , and the Judge or other persons examining shall be entitled to receive from the person examined a fee of $5 for every examination. R. S. O. 1877, c. 141, s. 3.

INDEX.

    13

100

104